STUDIES IN HISTORY, ECONOMICS AND PUBLIC LAW

Edited by the

FACULTY OF POLITICAL SCIENCE
OF COLUMBIA UNIVERSITY

NUMBER 342

THE MOBILITY OF THE NEGRO

A STUDY IN THE AMERICAN LABOR SUPPLY

BY

EDWARD E. LEWIS

THE MOBILITY OF THE NEGRO

A Study in the American Labor Supply

BY
EDWARD E. LEWIS

AMS PRESS
NEW YORK

COLUMBIA UNIVERSITY
STUDIES IN THE
SOCIAL SCIENCES

342

The Series was formerly known as
Studies in History, Economics and Public Law.

Reprinted with the permission of Columbia University Press
From the edition of 1931, New York
First AMS EDITION published 1968
Manufactured in the United States of America

Library of Congress Catalogue Card Number: 68-58603

AMS PRESS, INC.
NEW YORK, N.Y. 10003

PREFATORY NOTE

THE writer is under obligation to a number of people for aid in connection with this study. The entire manuscript has been read and criticized by Professors John Maurice Clark and Frank A. Ross, of Columbia University, and by Messrs. O. M. Johnson and H. A. Turner of the Department of Agriculture. Valuable assistance has also been rendered by Professor Robert E. Chaddock of Columbia University, Professor Arthur F. Burns of Rutgers University, and Professor Abram L. Harris of Howard University. Miss Helen Schuldenfrei has helped in revising the manuscript. Editorial advice has been given generously by Miss Mildred Palmer and Miss Marie Butler. To all others who have from time to time rendered aid, the writer wishes to express his gratitude.

E. E. L.

HOWARD UNIVERSITY, MAY, 1931.

CONTENTS

FOREWORD

The Mobility of the Negro is the third volume to appear as a result of studies in the field of Negro Migration under grants by the Social Science Research Council and the Columbia University Council for Research in the Social Sciences.[1] It is an outgrowth of elaborate statistical explorations into the general subject with which the project has been concerned.

Ever since Reconstruction vast numbers of Negro agricultural workers in the southern states have been contributing regularly to the working populations of other sections. At times the movement has been greatly accelerated, at others retarded. Mr. Lewis, in selecting for particular study the period 1919 to 1924, has chosen an era in which years of considerable movement and years of lessened displacement both occur. A less important though influential factor was the fact that a larger mass of factual material exists for these years than for any other period.

The study is primarily methodological, its contribution being considerably beyond a mere description of what occurred in the five years treated. Concentrating on the economic factors underlying migration, Mr. Lewis has established techniques for determining the economic " push " of agricultural depression in the Cotton Belt and the eco-

---

[1] The other two are:

> *The Negro Peasant Turns Cityward*, by Louise V. Kennedy, Columbia University Press, 1930; and
> *The Negro in Modern Industrial Society*, by Dean Dutcher, Science Press, Lancaster, Pennsylvania, 1930.

nomic "pull" of industry in the North. This is done by logical classification of material and by graphic devices. By statistical and mathematical procedure it becomes possible to measure the relative effectiveness of the propulsive and attractive factors during different parts of the period. Finally, the conclusions reached by these methods are checked by historical analysis.

These techniques are applicable to other periods and other problems, though certain of the data requisite for the fullest analysis are at present available only for the period treated.

FRANK ALEXANDER ROSS.

CHAPTER I

THE PROBLEM—ECONOMIC FACTORS IN NEGRO MIGRATION

DURING the past fifteen years the supply of new industrial labor in this country has been considerably different from that of the pre-war period. Because of the restrictions imposed first by the War and then by the quota laws, the contribution of the European immigrant has been relatively small. In the place of these foreign-born recruits a large body of native workers has appeared; the general movement of population from farms and small towns to urban centers has provided American industry with a fresh labor reserve. The existence of such a reserve is a matter of considerable importance for both capital and labor. The industrialists find in an ample and easily accessible source of supply the means of expanding operations, and of controlling the wage level—" labor troubles " become less serious when an abundance of new workers can readily be pressed into service. Workers already in industry find the labor reserve the cause of keener competition for jobs and of a weaker bargaining position.

The probable number of laborers which this reserve will contribute to the future labor supply of the country, then, is of great interest to each class in the industrial structure. The contribution depends in part upon the number of people in the country who might be called upon to enter industry or, in other words, upon the size of the potential reserve. It depends also upon the conditions under which the transfer of workers actually takes place. A study of the causes of the movement of workers into industry is likely to furnish a clue to the future role of the new reserve in the labor supply of the country. This essay is concerned with the causes of the movement of one very important element in the reserve—the southern Negro. Through the migration of the southern Negro to urban centers, a large body of workers has been added to the ranks of industrial labor. The movement is important, however, not only because of the number of workers involved, but also because of the special racial problems which it has created.

The object of this investigation has been to estimate the relative importance of certain factors in the movement of the southern Negro into industry. Specifically, the "pull" of industrial demand for labor has been compared with the "push" of agricultural disorganization in the Cotton Belt. Did the Negro answer the call for industrial workers regardless of the conditions which he was leaving? Or did he move away from the unfavorable conditions of the South whether or not he was needed in industry? Perhaps the explanation [1] of his movement is to be found between the extremes set by these questions. Our expectation as to the

[1] Attention is devoted in this essay exclusively to economic factors. The boll weevil is featured, and lynching ignored. It should be pointed out that in treating negro migration from an economic standpoint, it is not assumed that the movement is solely an economic phenomenon.

In this movement there are two sets of causes which might be described by the term "social." The first is the racial discrimination characteristic of all parts of the Cotton Belt—the Jim Crow laws, poor schools, lynchings actual or potential, and the general technique of keeping the Negro aware of his inferior position. The second set of causes are those forces which may be summed up in the phrase, "the lure of the city." In spite of the existence, and perhaps the great importance, of these social factors, it is possible to study the economic factors alone, because the social factors are relatively uniform throughout the Cotton Belt, and because social conditions are relatively unassociated with agricultural disorganization or industrial demand for labor.

part to be played by the southern Negro in the industrial labor market depends to a considerable extent upon the answers to these questions. Certain phases of the recent southern agricultural situation are not likely to be reproduced. In the years immediately following the War the spread of the boll weevil over the Cotton Belt was completed. The first period of drastic readjustment has passed. The boll weevil will tend to become less of a disorganizing factor in cotton production and therefore less of a force in the movement of the Negro. The relative influence of this changing agricultural situation and of the industrial factor must be estimated in order to gain a basis for judging the future importance of the Negro in the industrial labor supply of the country.

Whatever the importance of the problem which has just been stated, the question arises whether the industrial and agricultural factors are too complex for fruitful study. It is a principle of scientific procedure that the elements of a problem should be reduced as far as possible to simple, homogeneous quantities. Are we justified, then, in taking as two of the main elements of this investigation, agricultural and industrial conditions?

The industrial demand for labor, consisting of the number of workers absorbed, or rather desired, by industry, is of itself a homogeneous entity. Diversity appears in the channels by which such a demand is transmitted—that is, in the processes by which the demand is transformed from a potential to an actual influence on men's actions. Industrial labor demand as a factor in migration showed variations throughout the Cotton Belt, because of the differential effectiveness of the means by which this demand was communicated to the various regions. Whatever these channels of communication may have been, however, the factor itself remained the same—namely, the prospects of a given economic status to be attained by entering industrial employment.

It is illuminating to compare the problems involved here with those of Dr. Dorothy Thomas in her study [1] of the emigration from England to the United States. She was able to get a rough index [2] of the labor demand of American industry, because she was studying temporal fluctuations for a whole country rather than geographical variations within a country. As a measure of the " pull " of American industry on the people of England, however, this index falls short of perfection because of the same deficiency of data which prevents us from constructing any direct index at all. For the " pull " of American industry in England depends not only upon the need for workers in the United States, but also upon the personal connections, attitude of the press, recruiting activities, and other means by which the need for workers was conveyed to Englishmen. To take another illustration, the effect of any given degree of labor demand in the United States became progressively greater in Italy during the period from 1890 to 1914, as the " newer " type of immigrant established himself in America, and began to urge his compatriots to make the same move. The conclusion to be drawn from the foregoing considerations is not that the " industrial factor " of Dr. Thomas' study and of the present investigation is too complex in character to lend itself to scientific analysis, but simply that the problem of measuring the factor is one of very great difficulty.

In contrast to the industrial factor, " agricultural conditions " seem to present both the impossibility of measurement, and the more serious problem of underlying complexity. Whereas the industrial factor is composed of a single

[1] Dorothy Swaine Thomas, *Social Aspects of the Business Cycle*, 1927, pp. 147-51.

[2] Namely, the degree of industrial activity.

quantity, the demand for industrial labor, the agricultural factor includes a number of distinct elements—boll weevil damage, soil exhaustion, price fluctuations, and others. In spite of its composite structure, the agricultural factor may be regarded for our purpose as a single entity. Agricultural conditions in general, and each particular element, are important in the migration of Negroes solely because they influence the expectation of future income on the part of the individual. Such expectation is chiefly conditioned by the income of the immediate past and also by the more elusive influences upon men's economic judgments. Any study of the economic factor must include both types of influence.

In the Cotton Belt, the two chief influences upon the expectation of income on the part of farmers are the income actually received, and the peculiar " psychological " reaction to which the presence of the boll weevil typically gave rise, at least during the first seasons after its arrival.[1] The agricultural factor, therefore, is made up of two components—the amount of income actually received by cotton growers and the psychological effects of the boll weevil, which not only reduces income but seems to inspire rather more pessimism than other types of income losses. However one might wish for a complete analysis of each component separately, it is not only necessary but proper to study the combined action of the two, for several reasons. First, the totality of influences upon the expectation of income in the South is the only factor which can properly be compared with the industrial demand for labor. Second, concerning behavior of this composite factor as a whole we have information enough to enable us to draw certain important conclusions. Third, any other attack upon the problem, even with complete data, meets with the very same logical complexity, for such an attack would involve the study of the

[1] For a brief discussion of the effects of the boll weevil, see p. 115.

influence of boll-weevil damage on migration. Even if full figures concerning boll-weevil damage were available, the effects of loss of income could not be distinguished from the more elusive psychological influence of the boll weevil upon the reaction of individuals to the general economic environment. While the factor—damage from the boll weevil —would be a single measured quantity, in its causal aspects it would be quite as complex as the " agricultural factor." [1]

The movement of the southern Negro is most advantageously studied by concentrating upon the short, post-war

[1] It is worth while, perhaps, to cite from other fields two examples of factors which are definitely measurable, but which show varying degrees of complexity in their causal aspects. The first example is that of supply as a factor in price, and the second, income as a factor in infant mortality. To say that the supply of cotton influences its price immediately opens the way for an analysis of the effect of acreage, weather, the boll weevil, changes in technique, and other conditions on price. A satisfactory analysis of the price of cotton involves the study of all these elements, for in a sense " supply " represents merely a certain group of factors. But supply itself may be taken as the ultimate term in a given problem not only because data may be available concerning it rather than its constituents, but because the amount of cotton offered for sale is the immediate determinant of price, no matter whence the cotton came. The underlying factors all converge upon the supply, and lose their identity in it.

The case is somewhat different with the economic factor in infant mortality. Low income carries with it not only the inability to purchase proper medical service, but also such conditions as ignorance of the importance of pre-natal care, employment of mothers during pregnancy, and employment of mothers after the birth, resulting in a reduction in breast feeding and the transfer of general care to the less competent hands of older children. Low income is therefore a significant factor in infant mortality because it is associated with a number of influences on the health of babies.

If the only influence upon the expectation of income were actual income, then the agricultural factor would be strictly analogous to supply, for all the constituent elements would converge upon the income received, and each would be effective only insofar as it affected income. Since, however, the agricultural factor must include not only income, but a psychological influence which happens to be associated with variations in income, it resembles the economic factor in infant mortality.

period from 1919 to 1924. This period is best suited to a study of the problem for several reasons. A study of the migration which occurred during the War would be likely to have little significance for peace-time conditions. A larger body of systematic information is available for the years from 1919 to 1924 than for any other period. The study of this interval is significant from the standpoint of the agricultural and industrial factors as well. With regard to industry, the demand for labor fluctuated, reaching high points in 1920 and 1923, and a low point in 1921. As to the agricultural factor, profound changes occurred in the South which were reflected in the slow westward movement of the Cotton Belt—the opening of the new cotton land in western Texas and New Mexico and the decline of cotton raising in Georgia and South Carolina. Thus the investigation is limited to the five-year period from 1919 to 1924 both because the data are available for that period only and because its particular interest would make it a profitable object of study even if data were available for other periods. The significance of this limited investigation for the broader problem of Negro migration as a whole will be discussed in the concluding chapter.

The rôle of the agricultural and industrial factors must be discussed briefly before our major problem can be presented more definitely. Viewing the situation as a whole, the problem of the agricultural and industrial factors in the movement of the Negro may be regarded as that of agricultural " push " and industrial " pull." Conditions in the Cotton Belt during the period studied were generally bad, and industrial labor demand was quite strong. As a result, the evidence indicates that in 1924 there were fewer Negroes in agriculture than in 1919. A detailed analysis, however, reveals the fact that in parts of the Cotton Belt the number of Negroes in agriculture increased from 1919 to 1924. Neither industrial labor demand nor agricultural difficulties will explain these increases. The agricultural factor, however, may be interpreted in such a way as to imply either favorable or unfavorable agricultural conditions, while industrial demand may be similarly regarded as positive or negative; i. e., as drawing workers away from rural territory or forcing them back through urban unemployment. This broader interpretation of the two factors enables us to explain the local increases in the number of colored agricultural workers. Even if there were no areas of increase, it would be necessary to take account of the full range of both factors, for in the case of a decrease, one could not assume outright that agricultural conditions were bad and also that industrial demand was positive. The given decrease might have been the result of a very strong labor demand in the face of good agricultural conditions, or it might have been the result of bad agricultural conditions at a time when there was considerable immigration into rural districts because of the lack of industrial opportunities. In short, the movement of the Negro must be regarded as the net result of either favorable or unfavorable agricultural conditions, and of either positive or negative labor demand.

A straightforward attack upon the problem of this investigation would involve the measurement of three elements; namely, the movement of the Negro population, agricultural conditions, and industrial demand for labor. With adequate measures of these three quantities, the ordinary technique of correlation could be applied, and the relative importance of the industrial and agricultural factors could be estimated directly. It is impossible, however, to obtain such indexes for all three quantities. The first presents comparatively little difficulty, for while good statistics of migration are lacking, it is possible to resort to satisfactory approximations. It should be apparent, however, from the foregoing discussion of the agricultural and industrial factors, that direct measurement is out of the question. One must, therefore, proceed by indirection.

While it is impossible to measure the industrial and agricultural factors, we have extensive information concerning three distinct phenomena which are influenced by them. The operation of these factors is reflected not only in the movement of the Negroes, but also in the movement of the whites, and in changes in the amount of cotton cultivated in the various parts of the Cotton Belt.[1] Moreover, the underlying factors did not enter into these phenomena to the same degree. It happens that during the period studied, the industrial factor was apparently considerably more important in the movement of the colored farmers than in the movement of the whites. This differential serves to uncover the underlying factors in the following manner. The closeness with which any two of the three resultant phenomena are associated depends on the importance of the factors common to both. It is possible, therefore, by making a detailed comparison of association among the three phenomena—white and colored population movements and changes in the scale of cotton cultivation—to infer much concerning the underlying forces. This general procedure, the study of the differential closeness of association exhibited by the three resultant phenomena—characterizes the statistical part of the investigation. It may be added that while the data of the problem concern conditions in the Cotton Belt only, this does not mean that any emphasis in the analysis is given the agricultural over the industrial factor. For the changes in the Cotton Belt which are studied arose both from the agricultural conditions and from industrial labor demand.

---

[1] The changes in the amount of cotton cultivated may be the result of the agricultural factor, i. e., of conditions such as boll weevil damage, and also the result of the industrial factor, creating labor scarcity or labor abundance.

The advantages of a strictly statistical treatment of the problem are obvious, and need not be elaborated here. The chief disadvantage is that the thorough and satisfactory analysis which it makes possible can be applied only to a limited set of problems. The analysis of the extensive quantitative data concerning changes in cotton cultivation and in the number of Negroes and whites contributing to it is therefore supplemented in this investigation by a study of more general information. Much of it is in non-quantitative form, and the conclusions which one may draw from it are less precise or in any case more difficult to evaluate than the statistical results. On the other hand, one can take account of more aspects of the problem, and this broader view offsets the shortcomings of the analysis. The treatment also utilizes information concerning the entire period from 1919 to 1924, whereas the statistical data, taken from the United States Census of Agriculture, apply only to the first and last years of the period. In analyzing this supplementary material, then, one is able to study the temporal sequence of events and thus to throw more light on the causal relationships of the various elements of the situation. The essay includes a year-by-year study of the period, as well as the detailed statistical analysis of the net changes from the first year to the last. Both parts of the investigation represent merely different approaches to the same problem—the relative importance of the agricultural and industrial factors in the movement of the southern Negro into industry.

CHAPTER II

COTTON AND COLORED FARMERS

IN many parts of the South, striking changes in the amount of cotton cultivated occurred from 1919 to 1924. In some sections the area cultivated in 1924 was much greater than that in 1919, while in others it was much less. Marked changes also occurred in the number of Negro cultivators in various parts of the Cotton Belt. These two sets of changes were associated; sections which lost or gained in cotton even by a small amount tended to lose or gain in Negro population as well. This fact is to be explained in part by the demand for industrial labor, which drew such numbers of workers from the cotton fields that the planters were compelled to curtail their operations; or by industrial unemployment, which sent workers back to the agricultural regions, thus encouraging an expansion of cotton acreage. It is also to be explained in part by the difficulty of raising cotton profitably, which caused both the abandonment of its production and the emigration of Negroes who were left with no means of gaining a livelihood, or by favorable agricultural conditions, which caused the expansion of cotton acreage and at the same time attracted new workers into the region. By studying this association it is possible to estimate the relative importance of these two factors in the movement of the Negro.

Before such an analysis can be presented, the data which are used to measure the two sets of changes must be described. For cotton acreage, the United States Census of

Agriculture gives the desired information. Regarding the Negro, it is necessary to use the number of " colored " farmers [1] in the same Census to indicate the Negro participation in southern agriculture. An accurate index of changes in this participation [2] would take into account farm owners, farm tenants, and farm laborers. Of these, the Census data under the heading " farmers " include the number of farm owners and farm tenants only. Nevertheless, the figures are suited to the present purpose because they include " croppers," [3] who form in large measure a substitute for the agricultural wage laborers in the South. The number of agricultural workers who are not listed as " farmers," therefore, is small, and furthermore, the proportion of such workers did not change greatly from 1919 to 1924 in most parts of the Cotton Belt. [4] Because of these two considera-

[1] The actual figures available are the number of " colored " farmers rather than the number of " Negro " farmers. The two are for practical purposes equivalent, however, since there are very few of the other " colored " persons (Indians, Japanese, Chinese, etc.) in the region studied. The term " colored " farmer, is used throughout to denote the Census figures.

[2] There are no figures available by counties to indicate changes in the total agricultural population. The " farm population " figures for 1924 are not comparable with those of " rural population " for 1919. The figures for " farm population " for 1919 are given only by states.

[3] One finds the form of tenancy known as " cropping " only in the South. While the cropper cultivates a specific piece of land on a crop-sharing basis and thus may be classified as a farm tenant, work, animals, and equipment are provided for him, and his operations are subject to close supervision. From the standpoint of the requirements of capital and skill, therefore, the cropper is practically a farm laborer.

[4] One corollary of the fact that most of the work of southern agriculture is performed by " farmers " should be pointed out here, namely, the relative inflexibility in the amount of cotton which any one farmer can plant. The maximum acreage which can be raised depends upon the amount of labor available for picking the bolls, rather than upon the amount of labor required for cultivation. Except in the new western part of the Cotton Belt, the general practice is to

tions, the percentage of change in the number of colored farmers is a close approximation to the percentage of change in the number of colored agricultural workers. This, in turn, is for practical purposes an adequate index of the movement of the colored population into and out of the agricultural regions which are being studied.

With these preliminary explanations, it is possible to present the analysis of the association of colored farmers and cotton acreage.[1] The analysis follows three distinct modes of procedure. First an examination of the geographical distributions of the changes in cotton acreage and the shift in Negro population are compared. A few counties are then studied individually. Finally, the correlation is studied with the aid of a double-entry table. An analysis of this table prepares the way for the more detailed study presented in the following chapter.

rely for the most part upon the extra labor for picking which is available in the farmer's family. Large scale operation for individual farmers, such as is carried on by the western wheat farmer, is not generally found in the Cotton Belt. A minimum cotton acreage also exists. Since cotton is the one cash crop upon which money income, or credit for the advance of supplies, depends, a farmer must plant a certain minimum acreage in cotton in order to carry through the season's operations. Changes in cotton acreage may, therefore, be expected to be accompanied by changes in the number of farmers cultivating cotton.

[1] In this study the association referred to, namely that between changes in the number of colored farmers and changes in cotton acreage from 1919 to 1924, will be designated by the elliptic phrase, "the association of colored farmers and cotton acreage." Later, other associations will be designated by analogous phrases. For example, the association between the changes in the number of white farmers and in cotton acreage from 1919 to 1924 will be called "the association of white farmers and cotton acreage." In each one of the associations discussed, changes from 1919 to 1924 are treated. There is, therefore, no ambiguity involved in a phrase which leaves this common characteristic of the associations to be filled in by the reader.

ANALYSIS OF GEOGRAPHICAL DISTRIBUTIONS

The geographical distribution of the changes in the number of colored farmers is presented in Plate I on page 25.[1] Passing across the map from the counties in Virginia and North Carolina to the counties in Texas, rather marked regional differences appear. Of the counties in Virginia and North Carolina, all but two North Carolina counties were either stationary or increasing in number, and these two decreased less than 15%. In South Carolina only one county was stationary and the rest were decreasing, one losing more than 50%. In Georgia there was a rather consistent area of even greater decreases. The whole state of Georgia showed only two increasing and one stationary county, while a substantial proportion of the counties decreased more than 25% and a number more than 50%. West of Georgia a somewhat different situation prevailed. In Alabama, Mississippi, and stretching up into Tennessee, the counties were for the most part decreasing, but less violently than in the southeast. Of the 87 counties in these three states, none decreased as much as 50% and only five decreased more than 25%. Moreover, there were notable exceptions to the rule of prevailing decreases. Four counties in Alabama and one in Mississippi increased more than 15%, while Tennessee contained the county showing the largest increase in the sample. A few more counties increased between 5% and 15%, and a number were stationary.

The Mississippi River Valley, comprising the counties in eastern Arkansas, northwestern Mississippi and eastern Louisiana, showed on the whole rather greater decreases

---

[1] For the statistical study 238 counties in the Cotton Belt have been selected according to criteria which are stated in Appendix A. In general these consist of all the rural counties lying in that part of the Cotton Belt in which both cotton and the Negro were of importance, and fulfilling certain technical conditions demanded by the analysis.

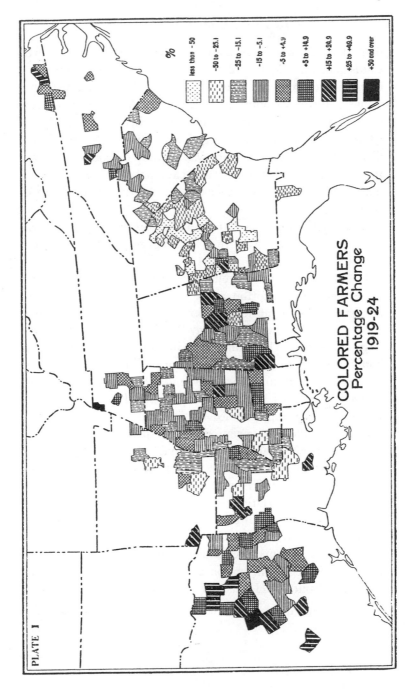

COLORED FARMERS
Percentage Change
1919-24

%

less than - 50
-50 to -25.1
-25 to -15.1
-15 to -5.1
-5 to +4.9
+5 to +14.9
+15 to +24.9
+25 to +49.9
+50 and over

PLATE 1

than those in the three states just discussed. In western Louisiana, outside the Mississippi River Valley, two parishes [1] increased more than 15% and a third remained stationary. Bradley County in southwestern Arkansas increased more than 15%. Texas presents two rather distinct regions. In the east, no county changed more than 15% in either direction. In the west, there was a group of counties showing consistent and, for the most part, pronounced increases. The latter group lay either in the Black Waxy Prairie region or near it.

The distribution of changes in cotton acreage is shown in the map on page 27. In it striking geographical characteristics are apparent.

Counties in North Carolina and Virginia showed rather large increases in cotton acreage. In contrast with these, almost all the counties in South Carolina and Georgia showed decreases, while in many the acreage was reduced by half or more. The counties losing more than half their cotton acreage were confined to Georgia. In Alabama some counties showed large increases and others large decreases. These two sets of counties were separated quite distinctly, the decreases being confined to the southwest. Mississippi showed considerable variation with respect to increases and decreases in cotton acreage, and no very definite geographical distribution of this variation. Even the Yazoo-Mississippi Delta which in many respects is of special interest in cotton raising showed variations which were not particularly consistent and not very different from the variations in the rest of the state. To the west of the Mississippi River, however, there was a region rather consistently made up of counties showing decreases in cotton acreage, although St. Martin Parish in southern Louisiana showed an increase of over

[1] In Louisiana the "parish" corresponds to the "county" of other states.

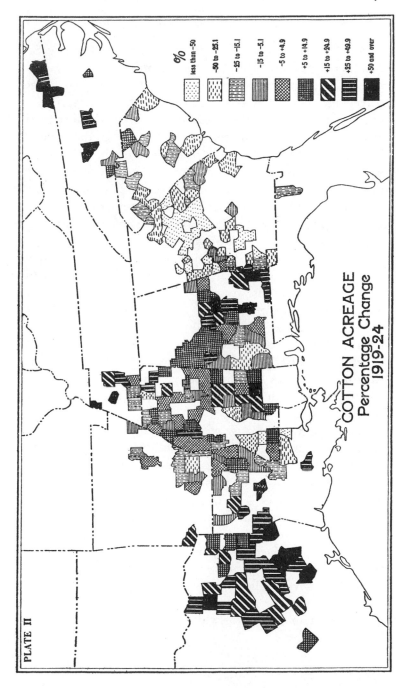

COTTON ACREAGE
Percentage Change
1919-24

%
less than −50
−50 to −25.1
−25 to −15.1
−15 to −5.1
−5 to +4.9
+5 to +14.9
+15 to +24.9
+25 to +49.9
+50 and over

PLATE II

25%. Unlike the other Mississippi Valley parishes, St. Martin devoted a comparatively small proportion of its acreage both in 1919 and in 1924 to cotton, and therefore the percentage changes in cotton acreage were not very significant. Three more of the Louisiana parishes which showed pronounced increases in cotton acreage lay in the general Red River section. Sabine Parish, which lies in the western part of the state on the Texas border, also showed increases of more than 25%. All the Texas counties showed increases of more than 5%, and most of them increases of more than 15%. These Texas counties formed the area of most consistent increases in the entire sample.

The county changes in cotton acreage, therefore, show a rather definite geographical distribution. The counties in Texas, western Louisiana, and Arkansas form an area of large and consistent increases. In the Mississippi Valley cotton acreage was generally reduced. The states of Mississippi and Alabama showed both increases and decreases which were distributed in a rather interesting manner. Georgia and South Carolina showed large decreasing areas and the states north of South Carolina showed, for the most part, increases.

When the two maps are compared, certain common characteristics are apparent. In the southeast both series showed a prevalent and considerable decrease. In Alabama and Mississippi there was more variation in each of the series than in other states. In these states, increases in cotton acreage occurred in more counties than did increases in the number of colored farmers. But in general the counties which showed an increase in the number of colored farmers are those which showed increases in cotton acreage. In the Mississippi River Valley there were, in general, decreases in both cotton acreage and colored farmers, and the counties of Louisiana and Arkansas which showed increases in either series usually showed them in both. In Texas most of the counties increased in cotton acreage, and increased or remained stationary as to colored farmers. All the counties in the Black Waxy Prairie section showed increases both in cotton acreage and in the number of colored farmers. Broadly speaking, therefore, the two sets of changes are related.

The analysis in terms of geographical distribution indicates that the forces operating may have varied in different sections of the Cotton Belt. In two regions, namely the southeastern states and the Mississippi River Valley, widely prevalent conditions tending toward decreases in both cotton acreage and the number of colored farmers evidently obtained. This suggests damage by the boll weevil which at least in its first stages characteristically affects large contiguous areas. It also suggests wholesale movements out of the territory rather than local migrations. From the standpoint of cause one might expect that a strong labor demand outside of agriculture would affect large areas rather than isolated counties. Thus in these two regions industrial demand and the boll weevil may have been important.

From the map it is apparent that in Texas there were widely prevalent increases in cotton acreage though there were less consistent increases in the number of colored farmers in the same area. It might be expected that a relative absence of boll-weevil difficulties, combined with a favorable price situation would result in the increases of acreage. The increases in the number of colored farmers may have been caused in part by a relative lack of demand for labor in other regions. In so far as any relationship is to be found between the two sets of changes in this region, it is not to be explained in terms of boll-weevil damage or of industrial labor demand. In the Mid-Belt region of Alabama and Mississippi, localized conditions — such as differential prosperity of cotton growing—were apparently of more importance according to the geographical evidence. The conclusion relevant to the present study of net changes is that the causal situation which gave rise to these net changes was of a complex sort with different causes predominating in different sections.

ANALYSIS OF COUNTIES SHOWING LARGEST CHANGES

It may be seen from Plates I and II that several of the counties showed marked changes in the number of colored farmers or in cotton acreage over the period from 1919 to 1924. With respect to cotton acreage, a number increased more than 50% and a number decreased more than 50%. Two counties increased more than 50% in the number of colored farmers, a few more increased more than 25%, while others decreased similarly. Though these areas were not necessarily typical—i. e. they may not show the elements of the common situation in magnified and therefore more easily discernible form—they do contribute to the discussion by setting forth certain aspects of the problem more sharply, and should therefore be studied individually.

COUNTIES SHOWING INCREASES

Table I presents information concerning the eight counties which increased more than 25% in the number of colored farmers. When the first two columns of Table I are compared, it becomes evident that in a majority of the cases the increase in cotton acreage is less than the increase in the number of colored farmers. In Lake county, Tennessee, for example, the number of colored farmers in 1924 was over three times as great as the number in 1919, but the cotton acreage increased only 64%. May this increase be regarded as commensurate with a very large increase in the number of colored farmers? It will be seen from the corresponding figure in the third column that, when both colored

TABLE I

PERCENTAGE INCREASES IN THE NUMBER OF COLORED FARMERS, IN COTTON
ACREAGE AND IN THE TOTAL NUMBER OF FARMERS, 1919-1924

FOR THE EIGHT COUNTIES IN WHICH THE NUMBER OF COLORED FARMERS
INCREASED MORE THAN 25 PER CENT

County	Colored Farmers (% Increase)	Cotton Acreage (% Increase)	All Farmers (% Increase)
Lake, Tenn.	217	64	53
Collin, Tex.	33	53	5
Harrison, Tex.	64	37	15
Hunt, Tex.	29	23	2
Travis, Tex.	46	10	38
Van Zandt, Tex.	34	28	2
Greensville, Va.	26	42	9
Sussex, Va.	35	24	19

Source of data: *United States Census of Agriculture.*

and white farmers are taken into account, the increase in
cotton acreage becomes greater than the increase in the total
number of farmers operating in the county. In terms of
changes in cotton acreage, therefore, as compared with
changes in the total number of farmers, the importance of
cotton in Lake county was rather greater in 1924 than it
was in 1919. A further inspection of the table reveals the
fact that in all of the counties except Travis county, Texas,
the increase in cotton acreage was greater than the increase
in the total number of farmers. With one exception, then,
the large increases in the number of colored farmers occurred in counties where the cultivation of cotton was in a
prosperous condition in the sense that it was increasing in
importance in the agricultural life of the county. It is also
apparent from Table I that in comparing the changes in the
number of colored farmers with the changes in cotton acreage one must take into account the number of white farmers
as well.

An examination of two of the counties listed in Table I

reveals a methodological problem. In Lake county, Tennessee, and to a somewhat less extent in Harrison county, Texas, there are very marked discrepancies between the magnitudes of the changes in the number of colored farmers and the changes in cotton acreage. The fact that these two counties show such large increases in colored farmers may be attributed principally to the method here employed for measuring these changes, namely, as percentages of the 1919 figures. In both of these counties the number of colored farmers in 1919 was relatively small. The result is that while the actual numerical increase in the number of colored farmers as compared with the total number of farmers was not great, the percentage increase was very large. This situation reveals the weakness of the percentage method used to take account of the varying size of counties. It should be said, however, that the alternative solution of the problem, in terms of the absolute numbers instead of percentages, would not only involve a much greater amount of detailed computation, but would give rise to analogous technical difficulties of just as serious a character.

The third county which is of special interest is Travis, Texas. In this county the increase in the total number of farmers was considerably greater than the increase in cotton acreage. This fact might be explained by a shifting of farm laborers in 1919 into farm croppers or share tenants in 1924. There is evidence that in Travis county an unusual amount of such shifting of status took place. The greatest increase in the number of colored farmers occurred in the cropper class. There was also an increase in the number of white croppers, probably because of a shifting of Mexican farm laborers into croppers. Moreover, there was a decrease in the average scale of operation in the county from 1919 to 1924. Such a decrease would indicate a decline in the amount of wage labor used per farm. Thus one **may** say that in Travis county there was probably a considerable reorganization of labor from a wage basis to a " farmer " basis between 1919 and 1924.

Discussion so far has been confined to counties showing large increases in the number of colored farmers. What happened in those counties which showed large increases in cotton acreage? There were twenty in which the cotton acreage of 1924 was more than 50% greater than the acreage of 1919.[1] In all of these counties there were either small increases or actual decreases in the total number of farmers, white and colored. The counties may therefore be considered as showing increases in the relative importance of cotton, as well as increases in cotton acreage.

A frequency distribution of changes in the number of colored farmers in these counties is presented in the second column of Table II. A comparison of this distribution with the distribution for all counties, as shown in the first column, indicates that the counties in which cotton growing was increasing markedly were much more likely to show increases in the number of farmers than the general run of the counties. On the other hand, if the distribution of the second column is compared with that of the third, for counties showing increases in cotton acreage less than 50%, less pronounced differences appear. Apparently the largest increases in cotton acreage take on an importance for the problem which is less than proportional to their magnitude. It will be further noted that whereas all of these counties showed increases in cotton acreage of more than 50%, eight of the counties showed increases in the number of colored farmers of less than 10%, and six more showed actual decreases. A somewhat asymmetrical relation is thus found here, in the sense that large increases in the number of colored farmers occurred usually in counties where cotton

[1] Some of these counties appear also in the group just discussed.

TABLE II

FREQUENCY DISTRIBUTIONS OF COUNTIES ACCORDING TO PERCENTAGE
CHANGES IN THE NUMBER OF COLORED FARMERS, 1919-1924

FOR ALL COUNTIES AND FOR GROUPS OF COUNTIES SELECTED ON THE BASIS OF
PERCENTAGE CHANGE IN COTTON ACREAGE

Per cent change	All counties	Counties with cotton acreage increasing more than 50 per cent	Counties with cotton acreage increasing less than 50 per cent	Counties with cotton acreage decreasing
over 60 ...	2	1	1	..
40 to 60	1	..	1	..
20 to 40	12	2	8	2
0 to 20	44	11	30	3
−20 to 0 ...	95	6	42	47
−40 to −20	57	..	10	47
−60 to −40	24	..	..	24
−80 to −60	3	..	..	3
Totals	238	20	92	126

Source of data: *United States Census of Agriculture.*

was definitely increasing in importance, but not all the counties which showed increases in cotton also showed corresponding increases in the number of colored farmers. Cotton
prosperity was apparently a necessary but not a sufficient
condition for the increase in the number of colored farmers.

The first of these results one might expect from the fact
that the colored farmer is so closely tied to the production
of cotton. The fact that the increase in cotton acreage is
not always accompanied by an increase in the number of
colored farmers may be explained by the following circum-
stance. Very large increases in cotton acreage may reflect
in certain cases shifts from other independent forms of agricultural activities. Such shifts would, of course, be of less
significance as far as population changes are concerned than
the expansion of the agricultural activity as a whole of a
given county.

TABLE III

CHANGES IN ACREAGE HARVESTED IN COTTON, AND CHANGES IN ACREAGE
HARVESTED IN ALL OTHER CROPS, 1919-1924

FOR ALL COUNTIES IN WHICH COTTON ACREAGE HARVESTED INCREASED
MORE THAN 50 PER CENT

*Counties in which cotton acreage harvested increased more than
100 per cent*

County	Cotton (1000 acres)	All other crops (1000 acres)
Davidson, N. C.	4	−19
Davie, N. C	3	−10
Polk, Tex.	18	− 9
Sabine, Tex	9	− 7
San Augustine, Tex.	16	−13
Trinity, Tex.	11	−12
Brunswick, Va.	7	−10
Mecklinburg, Va.	9	..
Sussex, Va.	8	−12

*Counties in which cotton acreage harvested increased from
50 per cent to 100 per cent*

County	Cotton (1000 acres)	All other crops (1000 acres)
Crenshaw, Ala.	25	−25
Elmore, Ala.	31	−21
Henry, Ala.	23	−17
Grant, La.	5	− 8
St. Martin, La.	6	11
Warren, N. C.	9	−15
Crockett, Tenn.	14	− 4
Lake, Tenn.	16	− 8
Southampton, Va.	9	−19

Source of data: *United States Census of Agriculture.*

The evidence bearing upon the shift from other forms
of agricultural activity into the cultivation of cotton is presented in Table III, in which the net changes in cotton acreage are compared with the net changes in the acreage in

all other crops. It will be seen that throughout the table the changes in acreage for non-cotton crops consist of decreases which are often greater than increases in cotton acreage. The increases in cotton acreage, therefore, represent a substitution for other crops rather than an expansion of the total activity of the various counties. The counties which show increases in cotton between 50% and 100% lie for the most part in the central portions of the Cotton Belt. For these counties, the total acreage figures are much less significant than for counties lying on the outer borders of the " old belt." [1] The evidence for the counties increasing in cotton acreage over 100% is somewhat more satisfactory. For these counties, lying either in the Black Waxy Prairie region of Texas or in Virginia and North Carolina, it is probably also true that the acreage changes indicate not only a substitution of cotton for other crops but often a further diminution of other forms of agricultural activity.

The significance of such a finding for the present problem is that where the cotton acreage increased considerably, the total amount of agricultural labor performed in the various counties remained relatively constant. Thus it seems probable that in those counties which showed high percentage increases in the amount of cotton acreage, and particularly those in which the increases in cotton acreage were more than 100%, the situation with respect to the relation between the changes in cotton acreage and changes in the number of persons performing the agricultural labor of the county was considerably different from the situation in most of the counties in the region under consideration. There is reason to believe that the changes in cotton acreage in these other counties were more or less closely accompanied by changes in the total agricultural activity of these counties. The

[1] Much acreage was counted twice because of the practice in this section of planting two or more crops in the same field.

argument here, of course, is in relative terms, for the counties which show increases in cotton acreage greater than 100% reflect conditions which existed to a less degree in other parts of the Belt. The principal significance of the discussion is that it furnishes some theoretical basis for certain manipulations of data which are technically necessary in other parts of the study.[1]

COUNTIES SHOWING DECREASES

What is revealed by the study of counties which had the largest decreases in the number of colored farmers and of those in which the cultivation of cotton was most reduced? It can be seen in the map on page 25 that the counties which lost more than half of their colored farmers were situated in the southeast, 14 being in Georgia and one in South Carolina. Three of the Georgia counties lost more than 60% of the number of colored farmers in 1919. In two of these counties the cotton acreage decreased more than 80%. The number of colored farmers decreased less and the total number of farmers decreased still less. In the third county, the acreage in cotton decreased only 40% but the total number of farmers decreased about half as much. In all three of these counties, therefore, the cultivation of cotton was decreasing not only absolutely but relatively to the change in total number of farmers. The same is true of each of the 11 other Georgia counties which showed decreases in the number of colored farmers of more than 50%. The major decreases in the number of colored farmers took place in counties where cotton cultivation was not only definitely decreasing but also decreasing in relative importance. In the South Carolina county in which the number of colored farmers decreased 59%, cotton acreage decreased only 44% while the total number of farmers decreased 49%. This

[1] See p. 45.

forms an exception, though not a particularly striking one, to the general rule.

In the 25 counties in which cotton acreage fell off more than 50%, the total number of farmers decreased less than 50% in each case, and therefore according to this criterion the relative importance of cotton was also decreasing. What happened to the colored farmers in these counties? Of the 25 counties, 11 lost more than 50% of their colored farmers during the period of 1919-1924. Eight more lost over 40% and 4 over 30%, 1 over 25% and 1 over 10%. It is interesting to note that the county which decreased only 13%, in spite of the decrease of 60% in cotton acreage, was situated not in the southeast but in the southern part of Louisiana.[1]

The evidence therefore points to the conclusion that decreases in the number of colored farmers were rather consistently associated with pronounced cotton depression in the sense that decreases in colored farmers usually occurred where cotton acreage was reduced, and that wherever there were decreases in cotton acreage colored farmers migrated. That is to say, there was a greater degree of symmetry in the relation between cotton depression and changes in the number of colored farmers than in the relation between increases in cotton acreage and increases in the number of colored farmers.

ANALYSIS OF DOUBLE-ENTRY TABLE

While each type of analysis so far pursued contributes to an understanding of the relationship between changes in cotton acreage and changes in the number of colored farmers, neither gives an adequate picture of the relationship. In the graphical comparison of the two sets of changes by means of Plates I and II (pages 25 and 27) a broad treat-

[1] Where more diversification may have been practiced.

TABLE IV

Double-Entry Table

SHOWING THE ASSOCIATION BETWEEN THE PERCENTAGE CHANGES IN THE
NUMBER OF COLORED FARMERS, AND THE PERCENTAGE CHANGES
IN COTTON ACREAGE, 1919-1924

		-100	-80	-60	-40	-20	0	20	40	60	80	100	120	140	Over 160	Totals
Percentage Change In Number of Colored Farmers	Over 100								I							I
	80															
	60							I								I
	40					I								I		2
	20				2	I	5	3						I		12
	0			I	2	15	12	7	2	I		2	I			43
	-20		I	2	11	33	26	9	8	I			3		I	95
	-40		3	12	22	11	7	2								57
	-60	2	10	11		I										24
	80	2			I											3
	Totals.	4	14	25	35	48	51	29	18	4	I	5	I	I	2	238

Source of data: *United States Census of Agriculture.*

ment of the problem is employed, the relationship for individual counties being rather completely obscured. The study of counties showing a large variation for the two series, on the other hand, involves a small group rather than the general run of counties and thus furnishes a less satisfactory basis for generalization. In the present section both of these faults are avoided in that each county is represented by the specific value of the change in cotton acreage and the change

in number of colored farmers, and at the same time the total
number of counties are considered.

When the entire set of counties is put into a double-entry
table as in Table IV, it becomes evident that a general trend
of relationship exists between the changes in cotton acreage
and the changes in the number of colored farmers. Counties which showed decreases in one of the variables also
showed on the average decreases in the other variables.
Counties which showed increases in cotton acreage showed
either increases in colored farmers or small decreases. This
results in an upward trend from left to right. From examination of the rows of the distribution rather than the
columns, the same conclusion as to the association of the
two variables may be drawn.

An inspection of the distribution indicates, however, a
rather marked difference between the association among
counties showing increases in cotton acreage and those
showing decreases in cotton acreages. A comparison of that
part of the table which lies to the left of the vertical zero
line with that part which lies to the right of this line shows
that the upward trend is much more pronounced on the left,
that is, for decreasing cotton acreage, than on the right.

The fact that a close association exists between decreases
in cotton acreage and changes in the number of colored
farmers points to the conclusion that decreases in cotton
acreage did not represent mere shifts into other forms of
agricultural activity, and decreases in the number of farmers
did not represent mere shifts into the labor status. The
conclusion is somewhat weakened by the fact that there
exists some tendency for other forms of agricultural activity
to be carried on in the South more by a regular labor system
than by a traditional tenancy system. Quite possibly the
association between decreases in the number of farmers and
decreases in cotton acreage might reflect to some extent a

change in crop organization with an accompanying change in labor organization. The magnitude of the decreases, however, together with evidence of the rather small proportion of independent agricultural activities in the South, even at the end of the period, points to the first interpretation of the relationship noted.

In the case of counties showing increases in cotton acreage the lack of relationship between changes in cotton acreage and changes in the number of colored farmers is to be explained in terms of the differential importance of the agricultural and industrial factors in these counties; a point which will be discussed more fully in another connection.

CHAPTER III

COMPARATIVE STATISTICAL ANALYSIS

In the last chapter, the association of changes in the number of colored farmers and changes in cotton acreage from 1919 to 1924 has been studied by means of three methods—comparison of the respective geographical distributions, discussion of certain individual counties, and examination of a double-entry table. These methods were adequate to establish the association, but a further analysis of the problem of the relative importance of the agricultural and industrial factors in the migration of Negroes calls for a selection of groups of counties among which groups there is reason to believe that the relative importance of the underlying factors varied, and for a comparison of the associations found in these groups.

In order to make these comparisons with any degree of accuracy, it is necessary to have a precise descriptive measure of the closeness with which the two series are associated. The fundamental concept of association indicates what this measure should be. Two variables are said to be associated if the value of one variable increases our knowledge of the value of the other. And the amount by which our knowledge is increased measures the closeness of the association. A precise measure of this increase in knowledge is found in the proportion by which the range of uncertainty of one variable is narrowed by a knowledge of the value of the other.

The point may be illustrated by reference to Table IV. If in a given county the cotton acreage showed an increase

42

of between 20% and 40%, then the change in the number of colored farmers was somewhere between a decrease of 40% and an increase of 80%.[1] In other words, a knowledge of the change in cotton acreage in this county tells us that the change in number of colored farmers lies somewhere in the 120% interval from —30% to +40%. If we had no information of the change in cotton acreage, all we would know of the change in the number of colored farmers would be that it lay somewhere between a decrease of 80% and an increase of 80%, that is, somewhere in a 160% interval if we ignore for the moment the county with largest increase in farmers. For this is the range of changes in number of colored farmers for all the counties, as shown by the column at the extreme right of the table. The knowledge of the change in cotton acreage, therefore, has reduced the range of uncertainty for the other variable from 160% to 120%, a reduction of one-quarter of the larger range.

The measure of association used in this study consists of a percentage figure which indicates the proportion by which the range of uncertainty for one variable is reduced by a knowledge of the other; that is, the proportion by which our knowledge of one variable is increased by information concerning the other. Since one figure is required to describe a whole association, it is necessary to take the average reduction for the various columns,[2] for this reduction

---

[1] This can be seen examining the column which contains all the counties having the given change in cotton acreage, namely, the third column to the right of the vertical zero line.

[2] We might have used the rows of the tables instead of the columns, that is, asked how much a knowledge of the change in number of colored farmers added to our knowledge of the change of cotton acreage. It happens that, because of the nature of the measure used, the same percentage figure for the whole association is obtained, whether we start with the columns or the rows. Needless to say, there is no causal implication in the present procedure of estimating the change in number of colored farmers from a knowledge of the change of cotton acreage.

varies from column to column. For example, if a county showed a decrease in cotton acreage of 40% to 60%, the table shows that the range of uncertainty is reduced to that between a decrease in the number of colored farmers of 60% and no change at all.[1] The range of uncertainty is thus reduced from a total of 160% to a smaller range of 60%, representing a percentage reduction of about two-thirds in contrast to that found for the other column. Further variations are found in other columns, hence the necessity of taking an average for the entire table.

The average percentage reduction in the range of one variable arising from the knowledge of the other, is essentially the measure [2] by which the closeness of various associations is indicated in this study and therefore by means of which the associations are compared. For convenience, the measure is indicated in this study by the two letters PR standing for " percentage reduction."

One further methodological problem must be discussed before the actual analysis is presented. Among the counties classified in Table IV, there are a number which lie well away from the main body of the data. Most of these show very large increases in cotton acreage without corresponding changes in the number of colored farmers. Two counties show comparatively large increases in the number of colored farmers but only moderate increases in cotton acreage. The presence of these outlying cases destroys the significance of any descriptive measure computed for the distribution as a

---

[1] See the third column to the left of the zero line.

[2] The measure actually used only approximates this average, but does so sufficiently closely for the purpose. It is derived from the ordinary Pearsonian coefficient of correlation. The ratio of the reduced range to the total range is approximately equal to $Sy /\sigma y$. This in turn is equal to $\sqrt{1-r^2}$, therefore, the percentage by which the range is reduced is equal to $(1 - \sqrt{1-r^2}) \times 100$. In the case of a normal surface, this measure is equal to the average discussed above.

whole since they make a descriptive measure, such as the percentage reduction in scatter, "unstable" in the sense that its value is affected to an appreciable degree by the presence or absence of these few cases. These considerations are particularly important in view of the procedure which is carried out here, namely, that of comparing the relationship within various small groups of counties, for the inclusion of one or two of these cases, within a given group, renders a comparison with another group meaningless.

The elimination of these troublesome cases may be justified on both theoretical and technical grounds. Some theoretical basis for eliminating the counties in question may be found in the discussion of these counties carried on in the preceding chapter.[1] In counties showing the largest increases in cotton acreage, there was apparently a rather more pronounced shift into cotton production from other independent forms of agricultural activity than in other parts of the Cotton Belt. In so far as this is true, these counties may be regarded as presenting a different situation with respect to the relation between changes in cotton acreage and changes in the number of farmers raising the crop. As to the counties showing unusually large increases in the number of farmers as against cotton acreage, it will be recalled that in one of these (Travis, Texas) there was evidence of a considerable change from the use of wage labor to the use of cropper labor. Quite aside from the theoretical justification for these eliminations, there are certain technical considerations which make it legitimate to carry through the analysis after excluding these cases. A description of the distribution in Table IV, disregarding the outlying cases, may be justified by the same logic as that underlying the use of a median, which takes little account of a few very large or very small items in a frequency distribution.

[1] See pp. 30-37

In spite of these extreme cases, it is evident from the distribution of the table that most of the counties show a pronounced tendency toward a relationship between the changes in cotton acreage and the changes in the number of colored farmers. When small groups of counties are selected from the table and the relationship within a group is compared with that in others, the procedure of elimination becomes even more defensible. By selecting a group of counties which shows such a tendency with respect to the two series studied, and by classifying these counties according to some criterion such as the racial composition in 1919, significant conclusions may be reached.

In view of the foregoing theoretical and technical considerations, certain counties have been eliminated in the subsequent analysis. The actual counties eliminated include those showing an increase in cotton acreage of over 100%, the two counties which show relatively large increases in the number of colored farmers, and a few more, such as the remaining counties of North Carolina and Virginia, which were eliminated purely for reasons of convenience. These latter eliminations do not affect the conclusions, since a careful study of the various scatter diagrams show them to have no appreciable influence upon the value of the measures computed.[1]

THE ANALYSIS OF TABLE IV

An application of the methods which have been discussed in this chapter to the analysis of the two series in Table IV

---

[1] The counties eliminated are mentioned in Appendix C. In the case of a few distributions some counties have been eliminated which were included in others. This procedure can be justified on the ground that in those distributions from which the counties were not eliminated a study of the scatter diagrams shows them to have no appreciable influence upon the computed reduction in scatter. That is to say, the results would have been the same if these counties had been eliminated from all distributions in order to get an exactly comparable set.

TABLE V

MEASURES OF ASSOCIATION

BETWEEN PERCENTAGE CHANGES IN THE NUMBER OF COLORED FARMERS, AND
PERCENTAGE CHANGES IN COTTON ACREAGE, 1919-1924

For all counties and for several groups of counties

Group	Number of counties	Percentage reduction in variation (PR)
1. All counties......	238	18%
2. All counties except 20 eliminated because of "intstability"*............	218	37%
3. All with cotton acreage increasing	112	2%†
4. All counties with cotton acreage increasing except 20 eliminated	92	3%
5. All counties with cotton acreage decreasing	126	36%

Source of data: *United States Census of Agriculture.*

* See page 44 *et seq.*

† Not significant in the probability sense.

yields interesting results, presented in Table V. For the total set of 238 counties, the degree of association between changes in the number of colored farmers and the changes in cotton acreage is measured by reduction in scatter of 18%. When the eliminations mentioned have been made, the reduction in scatter for the remaining 218 counties is 37%. That is to say, on the average, the variation found in the columns or rows of Table IV is 37% less than the total variation for all the counties. Because of the fact, noted in the last chapter, that the association seems to be somewhat closer in counties decreasing in acreage than in counties showing increases in cotton acreage, the single figure 37% describes two different situations and is in the nature of an unrepresentative average.

In order to analyze the distribution of Table IV effectively, it is therefore necessary to divide the counties into those showing increases in cotton acreage and those showing decreases. The results of an analysis, based on such a division, are presented in the last three lines of Table V. For all counties showing increases in cotton acreage the reduction in scatter is 2%, which is not significant in the probability sense. Even with the elimination of outlying counties the reduction is only 3%, indicating a relatively loose association. For counties showing decreases in cotton acreage, however, the reduction is 36%. Thus the conclusions which were drawn in Chapter I concerning the relationship between changes in the number of colored farmers and changes in cotton acreage for all counties, for counties with increasing cotton acreage, and for counties with decreasing cotton acreage, are confirmed by the more elaborate analysis which has just been presented. The association in various groups of counties is now described by summary figures. The difference with respect to closeness of association between counties with increasing cotton acreage and counties with decreasing cotton acreage is indicated by the two reductions in scatter of 3% and 36%. The marked character of the difference between the two sets of counties is thus revealed.

COMPARISON OF COLORED WITH WHITE FARMERS

By employing the method of percentage reduction in scatter, it is possible now to compare the association of colored farmers and cotton acreage with a similar association of white farmers and cotton acreage. The percentage reduction in scatter for various groups of counties for this second association is presented in Table VI. In order to obtain a significant distribution for the changes in the number of white farmers, it is necessary to eliminate certain Mississippi River counties in which those changes were a

TABLE VI

Measures of Association

BETWEEN PERCENTAGE CHANGES IN THE NUMBER OF WHITE FARMERS, AND
PERCENTAGE CHANGES IN COTTON ACREAGE, 1919-1924

For all counties and for several groups of counties

Group	Number of counties	Percentage reduction in variation (PR)
1. All counties	238	2%†
2. All counties except 20 eliminated because of "instability"	218	3%
3. All counties except 20 bordering Mississippi River	218	6%
4. All counties except 20 bordering Mississippi River and 20 eliminated because of "instability"...............	198	8%
5. All counties with cotton acreage increasing	112	0%*†
6. All counties with cotton acreage increasing except 20 eliminated	92	0%*†
7. All counties with cotton acreage decreasing	126	5%

Source of data: *United States Census of Agriculture.*

* Less than one half of one per cent.

† Not significant in the probability sense.

reflection of a rather unique situation. The PR's after
these eliminations have been made are presented in the third
and fourth lines of Table VI, comparative figures for the
same groups and counties being presented in the third and
fourth lines of Table V.[1] It will be seen that for each
group of counties the association for white farmers is very
much less than for colored farmers.

For the total set of counties and for all counties with
increasing cotton acreage, the association between changes
in number of white farmers and changes in cotton acreage

[1] The last three lines of both tables are unaffected by these eliminations.

may be regarded as arising merely by chance. The same is true, as has been noted, of the association for colored farmers in all counties increasing in cotton acreage. With the elimination of the outlying counties, the first association, just mentioned, becomes significant. A comparison of the associations for colored farmers and for white farmers in counties with increasing cotton acreage reveals the fact that whereas the greater the increase in cotton acreage the larger the increase or smaller the decrease of colored farmers, the relationship for white farmers is of the opposite kind, the greater the expansion of cotton acreage the slighter the increase or larger the decrease of white farmers. In each case, the association is very slight; possibly the facts just discussed do not show any important tendency for the white farmers to behave differently from the colored when cotton acreage was increasing. The differential, however, between the two associations is maintained even where both associations are relatively loose.

The general conclusion that the changes in the number of white farmers were less closely associated with changes in cotton acreage than were those in the number of colored farmers has important implications as to the nature of the forces underlying the association for colored farmers. The indications are that those circumstances which were directly connected with the colored farmer were of more importance. Further light can be thrown upon these problems by a direct study of the changes in the number of white farmers.

The geographical distribution of the changes in the number of white farmers from 1919 to 1924 is presented in Plate III. The most striking characteristic of this distribution, as compared with that for colored farmers, is that no pronounced geographic pattern appears, with the exception of the region of large increases bordering upon the Mississippi River. Another characteristic of the map is that on

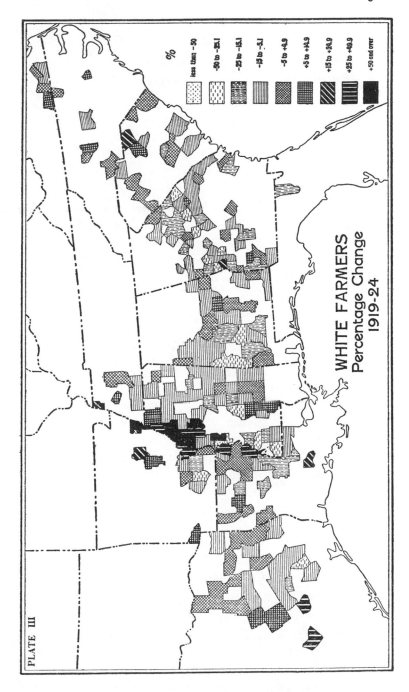

WHITE FARMERS
Percentage Change
1919-24

%
less than —50
—50 to —25.1
—25 to —15.1
—15 to —5.1
—5 to +4.9
+5 to +14.9
+15 to +24.9
+25 to +49.9
+50 and over

PLATE III

TABLE VII

FREQUENCY DISTRIBUTIONS OF COUNTIES ACCORDING TO PERCENTAGE
CHANGES IN THE NUMBER OF COLORED FARMERS, AND ACCORD-
ING TO PERCENTAGE CHANGES IN THE NUMBER OF WHITE
FARMERS, 1919-1924 (CLASSIFIED AS IN PLATES I AND III)

Per cent change	Counties with specified changes in number of colored farmers	Counties with specified changes in number of white farmers
Over 50	2	6
25 to 50	6	7
15 to 25	14	5
5 to 15	21	19
−5 to 5	39	62
−15 to −5	57	91
−25 to −15	42	34
−50 to −25	43	14
Less than −50	15	0
Totals	238	238

Source of data: *United States Census of Agriculture.*

the whole the changes in the number of white farmers seem to be considerably less violent than changes which have been found for the number of colored farmers. No county lost more than 50% of the number of white farmers in 1919 and relatively few lost more than 25%. A thorough comparison of the maps on pages 25 and 51 with respect to the actual magnitude of the changes is facilitated by Table VII, showing the number of counties which fall within each of the classes found in the maps. It will be seen that while no county lost more than 50% of its white farmers during the period, there were 15 which lost that proportion of their colored farmers. Further, while 43 counties lost between 25% and 50% of their colored farmers, there were only 14 losing that proportion of their white farmers. In the class showing decreases of 5% to

TABLE VIII

MEASURES OF ASSOCIATION

BETWEEN PERCENTAGE CHANGES IN THE NUMBER OF COLORED FARMERS, AND
PERCENTAGE CHANGES IN COTTON ACREAGE, 1919-1924

*For 238 counties classified on the basis of racial composition
of farmers in 1919*

Racial composition (Percentage of farmers colored)	Number of counties	Percentage reduction in variation (PR)
00.0 to 25.0	41	9%
25.0 to 37.5	47	19%
37.5 to 50.0	35	38%
50.0 to 62.5	47	22%
62.5 to 75.0	31	52%
75.0 to 100.0	37	27%

For 221 counties classified on the basis of racial composition
of farmers in 1919*

Racial composition (Percentage of farmers colored)	Number of counties	Percentage reduction in variation (PR)
00.0 to 25.0	33	14%
25.0 to 37.5	45	27%
37.5 to 50.0	35	38%
50.0 to 62.5	44	38%
62.5 to 75.0	31	52%
75.0 to 100.0	33	14%

Source of data: *United States Census of Agriculture.*

* 17 counties eliminated because of " instability ".

15% and in the class showing changes in either direction of
less than 5%, the frequencies are much greater for the white
farmers than for the colored. There are 153 counties—
considerably more than half—in these two classes mentioned
with respect to changes in the number of white farmers, but

TABLE IX

MEASURES OF ASSOCIATION

BETWEEN PERCENTAGE CHANGES IN THE NUMBER OF WHITE FARMERS, AND
PERCENTAGE CHANGES IN COTTON ACREAGE, 1919-1924

*For 238 counties classified on the basis of racial composition
of farmers in 1919*

Racial composition (Percentage of farmers colored)	Number of counties	Percentage reduction in variation (PR)
00.0 to 25.0	41	2% ‡
25.0 to 37.5	47	0% *‡
37.5 to 50.0	35	13%
50.0 to 62.5	47	9%
62.5 to 75.0	31	6%
75.0 to 100.0	37	4%

*For 211 † counties classified on the basis of racial composition
of farmers in 1919*

Racial composition (Percentage of farmers colored)	Number of counties	Percentage reduction in variation (PR)
00.0 to 25.0	36	14%
25.0 to 37.5	45	6%
37.5 to 50.0	33	8%
50.0 to 62.5	43	6%
62.5 to 75.0	29	8%
75.0 to 100.0	25	5%

Source of data: *United States Census of Agriculture.*

* Less than one half of one per cent.

† 27 counties eliminated because of "instability".

‡ Not significant in the probability sense.

only 96 counties with respect to changes in the number of colored farmers. The changes in the number of white farmers were, therefore, of relatively small magnitude, as compared with the changes in the number of colored farmers.

The problem of comparing the relations between changes in cotton acreage with the changes respectively in the number of colored farmers and the number of white farmers may be studied from a new angle by classifying the counties upon the basis of racial composition in 1919. The measures of association for such classes are presented in Tables VIII and IX. The first point upon which the tables throw light concerns the influence of the racial composition of the counties upon the differential closeness of the association found for the two races. Does the closer association for colored farmers, in counties in which they outnumber the white, arise merely because of this predominance?

If racial composition has a significant influence upon the degrees of association, then there should be a tendency toward a closer association between changes in number of colored farmers and changes in cotton acreage in those groups of counties with a higher percentage of colored farmers in 1919 and by the same token a looser association for the white farmers in the same group of counties. An inspection of Tables VIII and IX reveals the fact that although there is a tendency in the case of colored farmers for the association to become closer as the percentage of colored farmers increases,[1] the association for white farmers shows no opposite tendency to become looser. The evidence, then, would seem to point to the conclusion that differences which are found between white farmers and colored farmers are the reflection of conditions other than the predominance of colored farmers.

The material in Tables X and XI throw additional light upon the subject under discussion. For these tables, the

[1] This trend is curiously broken by a smaller reduction in scatter for counties with more than 75% colored population in 1919. This irregularity may be due to the fact that among these counties there are a number of Mississippi River counties where, as it is pointed out elsewhere, unusual increases in the number of white farmers occurred.

TABLE X

MEASURES OF ASSOCIATION

BETWEEN PERCENTAGE CHANGES IN THE NUMBER OF COLORED FARMERS, AND
PERCENTAGE CHANGES IN COTTON ACREAGE, 1919-1924

*For all counties with cotton acreage decreasing classified on the
basis of racial composition of farmers in 1919*

Racial composition	Number of counties	Percentage reduction in variation (PR)
More than half of farmers colored	78	40%
Less than half of farmers colored	48	20%

Source of data: *United States Census of Agriculture.*

counties with decreasing cotton acreage were divided into
two groups, one group consisting of counties having a majority of colored farmers in 1919, the other having a majority

TABLE XI

MEASURES OF ASSOCIATION

BETWEEN PERCENTAGE CHANGES IN THE NUMBER OF WHITE FARMERS, AND
PERCENTAGE CHANGES IN COTTON ACREAGE, 1919-1924

*For all counties with cotton acreage decreasing classified on the
basis of racial composition of farmers in 1919*

Racial composition	Number of counties	Percentage reduction in variation (PR)
More than half of farmers colored	78	8%
Less than half of farmers colored	48	0%*†

Source of data: *United States Census of Agriculture.*

* Less than one half of one per cent.
† Not significant in the probability sense.

of white farmers. It is to be noted here that the association
for both colored and white farmers tends to be closer in

counties having a greater proportion of colored cultivators. Thus the same result appears for groups of counties in which cotton acreage decreased in every county. From this evidence, it appears that the racial composition of the counties was of minor importance in the differential found for the two races.

The fact, then, that there is some systematic tendency for the relation of colored farmers to be closer in those groups of counties which have the greater proportion of colored farmers is to be explained probably not by these technical considerations but by the fact that there was some association between the proportion of colored farmers and the importance of cotton.

The classification of counties on the basis of racial composition yields further results, which support the conclusions already drawn as to the closer association for colored farmers than for white farmers. With one exception,[1] the differential is maintained in each group represented in the tables on pages 53 and 54.

ASSOCIATION OF THE CHANGES IN THE NUMBER
OF WHITE AND OF COLORED FARMERS

A comparison of the behavior of colored farmers and white farmers is not complete until the changes for these two are compared directly. The results of this analysis have a bearing upon the general problem of the relative importance of the agricultural and industrial causal factors. In so far as the two classes of farmers show a tendency to move together the factor which is likely to affect both races equally is to be given more weight. The reductions in scatter for the association between changes in the number

---

[1] In the group of counties having less than 25% of colored farmers (outlying counties eliminated) the associations for colored and for white farmers are equally close. For the significance of this fact see page 59.

TABLE XII

MEASURES OF ASSOCIATION

BETWEEN PERCENTAGE CHANGES IN THE NUMBER OF WHITE FARMERS, AND
PERCENTAGE CHANGES IN THE NUMBER OF COLORED FARMERS, 1919-1924

For all counties and for several groups of counties

Group	Number of counties	Percentage reduction in variation (PR)
1. All counties.........................	238	5%
2. All counties except 20 eliminated belcause of "instability"	218	5%
3. Asl counties except 20 bordering Mississippi River	218	16%
4. A l counties except 20 bordering Mississippi River and 20 eliminated because of "instability"...............	198	12%
5. All counties with cotton acreage increasing	112	3%
6. All counties with cotton acreage increasing except 20 eliminated	92	9%
7. All counties with cotton acreage decreasing	126	6%

Source of data: *United States Census of Agriculture.*

of white farmers and those in the number of colored farmers are given for various groups of counties in Tables XII and XIII. In each case the association is significantly positive but not very high as compared with the associations found for changes in cotton acreage and changes in the number of colored farmers. When the counties are classified according to the racial composition of the farmers in 1919, as in Table XIII, it is found that some of the associations are slightly closer than those found in groups of counties classified on other bases. It is interesting to note that two of the three closest associations appear in the two groups in which the colored farmers were more nearly equal in number to the white farmers. On the other hand, the closest

TABLE XIII

BETWEEN PERCENTAGE CHANGES IN THE NUMBER OF WHITE FARMERS, AND
PERCENTAGE CHANGES IN THE NUMBER OF COLORED FARMERS, 1919-1924

*For 238 counties classified on the basis of racial composition
of farmers in 1919*

Racial composition (Percentage of farmers colored)	Number of counties	Percentage reduction in variation (PR)
00.0 to 25.0	41	21%
25.0 to 37.5	47	7%
37.5 to 50.0	35	17%
50.0 to 62.5	47	16%
62.5 to 75.0	31	8%
75.0 to 100.0	37	7%

*For 234 * counties classified on the basis of racial composition
of farmers in 1919*

Racial composition (Percentage of farmers colored)	Number of counties	Percentage in reduction in variation (PR)
00.0 to 25.0	38	20%
25.0 to 37.5	47	7%
37.5 to 50.0	34	16%
50.0 to 62.5	47	16%
62.5 to 75.0	31	8%
75.0 to 100.0	37	7%

Source of data: *United States Census of Agriculture.*

* 4 counties eliminated because of " instability ".

association is found where the proportion of colored farmers
is the least. This last result may be the reflection of the
fact that in those sections where the colored farmers form a
small proportion of the total number of farmers, they re-
semble the white farmers more both with respect to the

general size of farms and the technical ability to carry on operations. The fact, already noted, that the associations for white and for colored farmers with the changes in cotton acreage are equally close in this group of counties where colored farmers formed less than 25% of the total number of farmers, points to the same conclusion.

An interesting fact appears when the association between changes in the number of white farmers and changes in the number of colored farmers in counties showing increasing cotton acreage is compared with the same association in counties with decreasing cotton acreage. The associations are practically equal for both groups, the counties with increased cotton acreage showing a slightly closer relation. The explanation for this may be that among the latter, shifts to cotton cultivation occurred without general expansions of agricultural activities and without corresponding changes in the number of farmers. Possibly under such circumstances outside influences affecting the two races differently, such as industrial demand for labor, were of less importance.

ANALYSIS OF GROUPS OF COUNTIES VARYING WITH RESPECT TO THE IMPORTANCE OF COTTON

While cotton occupies a dominant position as the chief cash crop of most sections of the Cotton Belt, the percentage of acreage devoted to cotton culture varies considerably. Even where the other crops raised do not bring any cash income, they spell somewhat greater self-sufficiency and hence greater independence of the fluctuations in the fortunes of cotton. It has been found desirable, therefore, to classify the counties according to the proportion of crop acreage devoted to cotton production.[1]   Groups of counties

[1] While the percentage of cotton acreage of itself does not afford a precise index of the importance of cotton, both because the acreage figures for all crops for 1919 are not very satisfactory and because the acreage in other crops may represent agricultural activity of varying independence of cotton, broad classes formed on this basis are significant.

TABLE XIV

MEASURES OF ASSSOCIATION

BETWEEN PERCENTAGE CHANGES IN THE NUMBER OF COLORED FARMERS, AND
PERCENTAGE CHANGES IN COTTON ACREAGE, 1919-1924

For 242 counties classified on the basis of the importance of cotton in 1919

Importance of cotton (Percentage of all crop acreage in cotton)	Number of counties	Percentage reduction in variation (PR)
00.0 to 25.0	25	25%
25.0 to 37.5	66	15%
37.5 to 50.0	66	38%
50.0 to 62.5	63	32%
62.5 to 100.0	22	51%

For 227* counties classified on the basis of the importance of cotton in 1919

Importance of cotton (Percentage of all crop acreage in cotton)	Number of counties	Percentage reduction in variation (PR)
00.0 to 25.0	20	20%
25.0 to 37.5	60	21%
37.5 to 50.0	64	44%
50.0 to 62.5	61	47%
62.5 to 100.0	21	62%

Source of data: *United States Census of Agriculture.*

* 15 counties eliminated because of "instability".

selected on this basis are represented in the tables on pages
61-3. The reductions in scatter have been computed for
changes in cotton acreage and for changes respectively in
the number of colored farmers, white farmers, and all farmers. For each of these associations two sets of measures
have been computed, one set of all counties and one set with
outlying counties eliminated.

THE MOBILITY OF THE NEGRO

TABLE XV

MEASURES OF ASSSOCIATION

BETWEEN PERCENTAGE CHANGES IN THE NUMBER OF WHITE FARMERS, AND
PERCENTAGE CHANGES IN COTTON ACREAGE, 1919-1924

For 242 counties classified on the basis of the importance of cotton in 1919

Importance of cotton (Percentage of all crop acreage in cotton)	Number of counties	Percentage reduction in variation (PR)
00.0 to 25.0	25	11%
25.0 to 37.5	66	6%
37.5 to 50.0	66	11%
50.0 to 62.5	63	8%
62.5 to 100.0	22	12%

For 218* counties classified on the basis of the importance of cotton in 1919

Importance of cotton (Percentage of all crop acreage in cotton)	Number of counties	Percentage reduction in variation (PR)
00.0 to 25.0	20	2%†
25.0 to 37.5	60	11%
37.5 to 50.0	64	12%
50.9 to 62.5	63	8%
62.5 to 100.0	11	61%

Source of data: *United States Census of Agriculture.*

* 24 counties eliminated because of "instability".

† Not significant in the probability sense.

It will be seen in Table XIV that both sets of associations show a systematic tendency to become closer as the percentage of cotton acreage increases. Even for the counties which show less than 25% of their acreage in cotton, the association of colored farmers and cotton acreage is fairly close.

TABLE XVI

Measures of Asssociation

BETWEEN PERCENTAGE CHANGES IN THE NUMBER OF ALL FARMERS, AND
PERCENTAGE CHANGES IN COTTON ACREAGE, 1919-1924

For 242 counties classified on the basis of the importance of cotton in 1919

Importance of cotton (Percentage of all crop acreage in cotton)	Number of counties	Percentage reduction in variation
00.0 to 25.0	25	27%
25.0 to 37.5	66	14%
37.5 to 50.0	66	31%
50.0 to 62.5	63	42%
62.5 to 100.0	22	46%

For 227* counties classified on the basis of the importance of cotton in 1919

Importance of cotton ∋ntage of all crop acreage in cotton)	Number of counties	Percentage reduction in variation
00.0 to 25.0	20	9%
25.0 to 37.5	60	25%
37.5 to 50.0	64	35%
50.0 to 62.5	62	41%
62.5 to 100.0	21	60%

Source of data: *United States Census of Agriculture.*

* 15 counties eliminated because of "instability".

The association of the white farmers shows no trend except that the adjusted measures for the counties with less than 25% cotton acreage are smaller than the other associations, while the association for counties with more than 62.5% is very high. For this latter group, however, so many counties had to be eliminated that the measure of

association is based on too few cases to be of much significance. A comparison of the tables on pages 61 and 62
adds weight to the conclusion that the colored farmers were
more closely related to cotton than the white farmers. The
adjusted reductions in scatter for the relation between the
changes in the number of all farmers and changes in cotton
acreage show slightly more consistently systematic variations
than those for changes in colored farmers. They are also
of about the same magnitude. The chief contribution, however, of this section of the analysis to the study is that the
relation between colored farmers and cotton acreage is relatively close even for counties showing small proportions of
cotton acreage.

CONCLUSIONS

The extensive statistical analysis of this and the preceding
chapters was undertaken in order to throw light upon the
relative importance of the industrial and agricultural factors
in the movement of the Negro. The bearing of the statistical results upon the central problem of the investigation
may now be pointed out.

The comparison of geographical distributions, as shown
in Plates I and II, not only established the general association of the two sets of changes for broad areas, but also
indicated that the causal situation underlying these changes
might be somewhat different in different parts of the Cotton
Belt. In two regions broad areas of prevailing decreases
were observed, indicating the presence of conditions such as
boll-weevil damage and industrial demand for labor. In two
other regions either consistent increases or a mixture of increases and decreases seemed to indicate differential agricultural prosperity among the counties.

The second conclusion reached from a study of the relation between changes in the number of colored farmers and

changes in cotton acreage concerns the differential results in counties in which cotton acreage was increasing, and those in which it was decreasing. The looser association for counties with increasing cotton acreage is in part due to the fact that these increases, especially when they were considerable, were achieved through the shifting from other independent forms of agricultural activity. But the large differential found between the association in the two sets of counties was also very likely the reflection of the differences in underlying causal situations. In the counties decreasing in colored farmers and cotton acreage, the association of the two sets of changes was the result of both the agricultural "push" and the industrial "pull." In the counties in which increases were noted, favorable agricultural conditions may have been accompanied by the so-called "negative" industrial factor, that is, the forcing of labor back to the farm because of urban unemployment. But this latter force was no doubt considerably less strong than the "positive" industrial factor, that is, the demand for labor.[1] The closer association for counties with decreasing cotton acreage arises then from the operation of the two strong industrial and agricultural factors, while the looser association for increasing counties arises from the operation of the strong agricultural factor and the relatively weak industrial factor.

A comparison of the association of colored farmers and cotton acreage with the similar association for white farmers for the same divisions, adds weight to the conclusion that in areas of decrease both the agricultural and the indus-

---

[1] The evidence presented in a later part of the study points to this conclusion. During the period from 1919 to 1924, there was a year or two of industrial unemployment, but the actual movement back into agriculture was not very great. That is, there was little migration due to the negative industrial factor. On the other hand, the same evidence shows that there were two periods of industrial demand for labor directly affecting the southern Negro.

trial factors were strong, but that in areas of increase in cotton acreage, the agricultural factor was of much more importance than the industrial, and further that other factors, such as crop shifting, were of considerable importance. The associations for both white farmers and colored farmers, in counties with increasing cotton acreage, are small even after the eliminations have been made, that for white farmers not being significant in the probability sense. If, as appears to be the case, the industrial factor was far less important in the migration of the white population during the period from 1919 to 1924 than in the migration of the colored population, the differential degrees of association for white and colored farmers in decreasing areas would seem to reflect the operation of both factors for the colored farmers and only one factor for the whites.[1] By the same token, the equal though small associations in areas of increase would seem to indicate the operation of the (common) agricultural factor alone. It should be emphasized that the point has to do merely with the contrast between increasing and decreasing areas, namely, that the relative importance of the two factors is different in the two. Whether the industrial or the agricultural factor was stronger in the decreasing areas, is another matter.

When the counties were grouped according to their racial composition in 1919, distinct differences were observed in the resulting association for cotton acreage and white farmers, and the corresponding association for colored farmers. The association for white farmers was lower than that for the colored farmers in all but one class. Since the industrial factor presumably affected the colored farmer rather than the white, the closer association for the colored farmers reflects the operation of the industrial factor as well as the

[1] Reasons for believing that the industrial factor was of small importance in the movement of the whites are stated on page 82. The statistical result cited immediately below adds weight to this belief.

agricultural. This finding adds weight to the conclusion that in the movement of the colored population, the agricultural and the industrial factors were of considerable importance, since the conclusion, which was reached for the total number of counties, is now found also to hold rather consistently among the small groups of counties.

A second interesting result may be derived from this part of the analysis. The association for colored farmers shows a distinct tendency to become closer in those groups of counties in which the colored farmers were of greater numerical importance. This result serves as a check upon the assumption which has been made as to the relative importance of the industrial factor for the two races. It has been assumed that the colored farmers were considerably affected by the demand for industrial labor, or the lack of it, but that the white farmers were to a much smaller degree affected. The lack of trend in the association for white farmers would seem to indicate the presence of the agricultural factor only in the movements of the white, for the following reason. The industrial factor affects the movements of farmers directly, but causes changes in cotton acreage only indirectly, through its effect upon the number of farmers available for cultivating the cotton. This being the case, if the industrial factor influences a given group of farmers, it will affect changes in the total cotton grown in the county more as the given group forms a greater proportion of the total labor supply of the county; that is, the changes in the given group of farmers will be more closely associated with changes in the total cotton acreage of the county if its numerical importance in the county is greater. One would expect, therefore, that if the industrial factor were of importance in the movement of the whites, the association for white farmers and cotton acreage would show a tendency to be closer in those groups of counties in which the white farmers were of greater numerical importance.

The operation of the agricultural factor, however, would not result in such a trend, since it affects both cotton acreage and the number of farmers directly. But effects may differ: The condition of cotton culture may cause an expansion or contraction of cotton acreage; it may also cause population movements into or out of the county. Whether there will be an actual migration, that is, whether the change in cotton acreage will be associated with a corresponding change in the number of farmers, depends upon the response of the population to the agricultural conditions. Do the farmers expand or contract the acreage of cotton according to good or bad agricultural conditions, or do they move into or out of the county as agriculture prospers or suffers? If any given group of farmers does respond by migrating, then changes in the number of farmers in that group will be associated with changes in the cotton acreage because of the agricultural factor. This is equally true of the group which forms a small or a large proportion of the population of the county. The degree of association of the changes in cotton acreage, and the changes in number in any group of farmers, in so far as this association arises from the operation of the agricultural factor, depends solely upon whether the response in that group is migration or change in acreage. The numerical importance of the group is irrelevant.

Thus if the industrial factor causes a trend in the association for a given group of farmers and cotton acreage, and if the agricultural factor does not cause such a trend, then, since the association for white farmers shows no trend, the assumption that only the agricultural factor influenced the white farmers is in accord with the facts. Furthermore, the assumption with respect to colored farmers, that is, that both the agricultural and the industrial factors were important, is borne out by the fact that a trend appears in the association for colored farmers. For such a trend, toward a closer association in groups of counties in which the colored farmers were numerically of greater importance, would be expected from the operation of the constant agricultural nexus of the two sets of changes, and the increasing industrial nexus.

The classification of counties on the basis of the importance of cotton in 1919 also throws light on the relative importance of the agricultural and industrial factors in the movement of the Negro. The association of the colored farmers was in each class (except the last, in which the number of cases was too small to give any reliable result) somewhat closer than that of white farmers.[1] This again indicates the influence of both factors, though here the influence of the industrial factor is rather minimized because of the fact that the differences in corresponding associations are not very great.

[1] While only one difference is significant in the probability sense, the constant signs of the differences add weight to the result.

CHAPTER IV

The Mathematical Treatment of the Problem

From a methodological standpoint, the problem of this investigation is of unusual interest. How far can one study factors for which numerical indexes, however approximate, are wholly lacking? In the foregoing pages certain general conclusions have been drawn concerning agricultural and industrial influences upon Negro migration. But no attempt has been made to approximate conclusions in the same form as those which could have been reached if direct information about the underlying factors were available. That is to say, no attempt has been made to estimate the actual measures of association between Negro migration on the one hand and the two underlying factors respectively on the other. Such estimates, however, can be made and it is the purpose of the present chapter to demonstrate this possibility. It may be noted that the methodological problem involved,—namely, the study of the " hidden " causes of observable phenomena, —is met in other fields and the technique developed here may therefore have an interest considerably beyond that of the particular problem which is being analyzed.

THE FUNDAMENTAL EQUATION

The three phenomena studied, — changes in colored farmers, in white farmers, and in cotton acreage, — were all influenced by the agricultural and industrial factors. In order to show how a knowledge of these three effects increases our knowledge of the underlying factors, it is necessary to set forth the relation of the two causal factors and the three resulting phenomena by means of schematic device.

70

Changes in the number of colored farmers in any county or in all the counties were due in part to agricultural conditions, in part to industrial labor demand or the opposite, and in part to a multitude of other factors. Let us state this same proposition in the form of an equation.

(1) (Changes in col-   (Were made   (Changes due to the
      ored farmers)   up of)   agricultural factor)
                                        (plus)
                                        (Changes due to the
                                        industrial factor)
                                        (plus)
                                        (Changes due to all
                                        other causes.) [1]

Equation (1) may be put into a slightly different form without changing its meaning. The changes due to any one factor may be thought of as the combined result of the strength of the factor and the importance to the individuals involved of that factor. The first term on the right-hand side of the phrase, " were made up of " in equation (1) may therefore be expressed as follows:

(2) (Changes due to the
      agricultural factor)   (were the result of)

          (The strength of   (Importance to
          the agricultural (times) colored farmers
          factor)   of the agricul-
                                   factor.)

---

[1] The equation cannot be interpreted in terms of individuals, it should be noted. If the item on the left of "were made up of" represents 100 farmers who migrated, it is not possible to split these up into two groups, 30, due to the agricultural factor and 70 to the industrial factor. Each migrant was presumably influenced by both factors. But the total percentage change in a county may be divided and attributed to the respective factors.

We may apply the same reasoning to the " industrial " term in equation (1) and rewrite the entire equation.

(3)   (Changes in colored   (equal)
                    farmers)

        Strength of agricul-   (Importance to colored
            tural factor)   (times) farmers of agricultural
                                                          factor)
                                                                          (plus)

        (Strength of indus-   (Importance to colored
            trial factor)   (times) farmers of industrial
                                                          factor)
                                                                          (plus)

                        (Changes due to
                        all other causes.) [1]

Equation (3) may be expressed in terms of the symbols conventionally used in correlation analysis. Let us denote the changes in the number of colored farmers by N, the changes in the number of white farmers by W, and the changes in cotton acreage by C. Further let the strength of the agricultural factor be represented by A, and that of the industrial factor by I, and the " residual " changes (i. e. those due to non-agricultural and non-industrial causes) by X with the appropriate subscript. Small r and σ, as usual, represent the correlation coefficient [2] and the standard deviation respectively.

[1] This last term is made up of the strength of the various factors times the importance of each respectively. Such a division is not made, however, for two reasons. Because the term includes more than one cause, the statements of relations within it would be complicated. The second reason is that in our analysis this term drops out because of certain of its characteristics. It is not necessary, therefore, to split it up into its component parts.

[2] It has been argued elsewhere that the degree of association is

In terms of these symbols Equation (3) becomes,

$$(4) \quad N = \frac{\sigma_N \, r_{NA} \, A}{\sigma_A} + \frac{\sigma_N \, r_{NI} \, I}{\sigma_I} + X_N$$

A comparison of the relative importance of the agricultural and industrial factors in the movement of the Negro involves a comparison of the relative closeness with which the changes in the number of colored farmers were associated with the two underlying factors. It is the specific object of the present chapter to make estimates of r_{NA} and of r_{NI}, which measure the two associations mentioned. In order to make these estimates it is necessary to analyze the relation of the two underlying factors to changes in the number of white farmers and to changes in cotton acreage.

SUPPLEMENTARY EQUATIONS

Corresponding to Equation (4) we may write another, expressing the relation of the changes in number of white farmers to the agricultural and other factors.

$$(5) \quad W = \frac{\sigma_W \, r_{WA} \, A}{\sigma_A} + \frac{\sigma_W \, r_{WI} \, I}{\sigma_I} + X_W$$

A similar equation may be set up for the changes in cotton acreage; for these changes are also due in part to agricultural conditions (which at the same time caused both changes in the number of farmers, and changes in the cotton acreage which they cultivated), in part due to the industrial factors (operating through the resulting abundance or scarcity of farmers to cultivate the cotton), and in part due to a multitude of other factors.

measured by PR, or the percentage reduction in scatter. It simplifies the mathematics, however, if during the discussion the degrees of association are indicated by the corresponding coefficients of correlation. This is legitimate in spite of the fact that these coefficients give a distorted picture of any association. For once the desired coefficients are found, they can be converted into the other measure before being interpreted.

$$(6) \quad C = \frac{\sigma_c \ r_{cA} \ A}{\sigma_A} + \frac{\sigma_c \ r_{cI} \ I}{\sigma_I} + X_c$$

Concerning the elements in equation (3), (4), and (5), we have certain information, namely, the associations between changes in colored farmers and changes in cotton acreage, between changes in white farmers and changes in cotton acreage, and between the changes in farmers of the two races respectively. Let us manipulate the equations into a form in which this information can be used.

DERIVATION OF THE FORMULAS

Multiply, term by term, Equations (4) and (5)

$$(7) \quad N \ W = \frac{\sigma_N}{\sigma_A} \ r_{NA} \ A \ \frac{\sigma_w}{\sigma_A} \ r_{wA} \ A$$

$$+ \frac{\sigma_N}{\sigma_A} \ r_{NA} \ A \ \frac{\sigma_w}{\sigma_I} \ r_{wI} \ I + \frac{\sigma_N}{\sigma_A} \ r_{NA} \ A \ X_w$$

$$+ \frac{\sigma_N}{\sigma_I} \ r_{NI} \ I \ \frac{\sigma_w}{\sigma_A} \ r_{wA} \ A + \frac{\sigma_N}{\sigma_I} \ r_{NI} \ I \ \frac{\sigma_w}{\sigma_I} \ r_{wI} \ I$$

$$+ \frac{\sigma_N}{\sigma_I} \ r_{NI} \ I \ X_w + \frac{\sigma_w}{\sigma_A} \ r_{wA} \ A \ X_N$$

$$+ \frac{\sigma_w}{\sigma_I} \ r_{wI} \ I \ X_N + X_N \ X_w$$

Let us next regroup the factors in the several terms of Equation (7) and sum.

$$(8) \quad \Sigma N \ W = \frac{\sigma_N \ \sigma_w \ r_{NA} \ r_{wA} \ \Sigma A^2}{\sigma_A{}^2} + \frac{\sigma_N \ \sigma_w \ r_{NA} \ r_{NI} \ \Sigma I \ A}{\sigma_A \ \sigma_I}$$

$$+ \frac{\sigma_N}{\sigma_A} \ r_{NA} \ \Sigma A \ X_w + \frac{\sigma_N \ \sigma_w \ r_{NI} \ r_{wA} \ \Sigma I \ A}{\sigma_I \ \sigma_A}$$

$$+ \frac{\sigma_N \ \sigma_w \ r_{NI} \ r_{wI} \ \Sigma I^2}{\sigma_I{}^2} + \frac{\sigma_N \ r_{NI}}{\sigma_I} \ \Sigma I \ X_w$$

$$+ \frac{\sigma_w}{\sigma_A} \ r_{wA} \ \Sigma A \ X_N + \frac{\sigma_w}{\sigma_I} \ r_{wI} \ \Sigma I \ X_N + \Sigma X_N \ X_w$$

We will assume that A, I, X_N, X_W, and X_C are all independent of each other, that is, that the sum of the products of any two,—e. g. $\Sigma A X_N$—is equal to zero.[1] Thus the terms containing such sums of products drop out of Equation (8). Further, if all variables are expressed as deviations from their respective means, $\Sigma A^2 = n\sigma_A^2$ and $\Sigma I^2 = n\sigma_I^2$ where n is the number of counties. Making these substitutions in Equation (8) and dividing through by n we get,

$$(9) \quad \sigma_N \sigma_W r_{NW} = \frac{\sigma_N \sigma_W r_{NA} r_{WA} \sigma_A^2}{\sigma_A^2}$$

$$+ \frac{\sigma_N \sigma_W r_{NI} r_{WI} \sigma_I^2}{\sigma_I^2}$$

Cancelling and dividing by $\sigma_N \sigma_W$ we get,

$$(10) \quad r_{NW} = r_{NA} r_{WA} + r_{NI} r_{WI}$$

Similarly, by multiplying Equations (4) and (6), we get,—

$$(11) \quad r_{CN} = r_{NA} r_{CA} + r_{NI} r_{CI}$$

And by multiplying Equations (5) and (6) we get,—

$$(12) \quad r_{CW} = r_{CA} r_{WA} + r_{CI} r_{WI}$$

The three quantities on the left of the equal signs in Equations (10), (11) and (12) are known. On the

[1] This assumption would seem to be very near the actual facts of the case. In the first place while there may have been some tendency for labor agents to seek out general regions of agricultural difficulty (that is, some tendency for industrial demand to be greater in regions in which the agricultural " push " was greater) this association was probably very slight, especially in the southeastern section of the Cotton Belt to which the analysis of this chapter is confined. For it was presumably impossible for labor agents to discriminate among the counties of Georgia and South Carolina with respect to agricultural conditions. The " residual " elements in the three equations are assumed to be unassociated among themselves and with the agricultural and industrial factors because of the fact that they arise from a large number of causes.

right side of the equal signs there are six quantities, each appearing twice; namely, r_{CA}, r_{CI}. r_{NA}, r_{NI}, r_{WA}, and r_{WI}. None of these is given by the available data,— they constitute six unknowns in the problem. Among these six we are interested in only two,—r_{NA}, indicating the association of the changes in number of colored farmers with the agricultural factor, and r_{NI}, indicating the associations of the same changes with the industrial factor. We must be prepared, however, to find all six in order to get rid of those which are not wanted. In order to solve for the six unknowns, three more equations must be added to the three already obtained.

For the moment, it is convenient to write down three equations which really postpone the issue, or rather, leave the way open for a number of different solutions. The first equation involves the relative importance of the agricultural factor in the changes in farmers of each race.[1] If we take k_A as a ratio between the two coefficients, r_{WA} and r_{NA}, we may write the equation

$$(13) \quad r_{WA} = k_A \, r_{NA}$$

The second equation is similar in form and concerns the relation between r_{NI} and r_{WI}

$$(14) \quad r_{WI} = k_I \, r_{NI}.$$

[1] Corresponding to the ratio of the two correlation coefficients is a ratio of the respective reductions in scatter. The latter ratio measures accurately the relative importance of the agricultural factor for the two races. Let the ratio of two PR's be h, and the ratio of the corresponding r's be k. Then it follows from the definition of PR that,

$$h = 1 - \sqrt{1 - k^2 r^2}/1 - \sqrt{1 - r^2}.$$

Hence the relation of h and k depends on the value of r. When k is given a definite value, however, h does not vary greatly. Therefore the assumption that k has a given constant value is practically equivalent to the assumption that h, or the ratio of importance, has a constant value.

A third equation expresses the relation of r_{CI} and r_{NI}.

$$(15) \quad r_{CI} = m \ r_{NI}$$

The three constants, k_A, k_I, and m will be discussed presently.

With the three equations originally derived, and the three equations just added, it is now possible to solve for the two quantities in which we are interested; namely, r_{NI} and r_{NA}. Let us first eliminate r_{WA} and r_{WI} by substituting Equations (13) and (14) in Equation (12) and then in Equation (10).

$$(16) \quad r_{CW} = r_{CA} \ k_A \ r_{NA} + r_{CI} \ k_I \ r_{NI}$$

$$(17) \quad r_{NW} = r^2_{NA} \ k_A + r^2_{NI} \ k_I$$

Then eliminate r_{CI} by substituting Equation (15) in Equations (11) and (16).

$$(18) \quad r_{CN} = r_{CA} \ r_{NA} + m \ r^2_{NI}$$

$$(19) \quad r_{CW} = r_{CA} \ k_A \ r_{NA} + m \ k_I \ r^2_{NI}$$

Divide Equation (18) by r_{NA}

$$(20) \quad \frac{r_{CN}}{r_{NA}} = r_{CA} + \frac{m \ r^2_{NI}}{r_{NA}}$$

Divide Equation (19) by $r_{NA} \ k_A$

$$(21) \quad \frac{r_{CW}}{r_{NA} \ k_A} = r_{CA} + \frac{m \ k_I \ r^2_{NI}}{r_{NA} \ k_A}$$

Subtract Equation (21) from (20)

$$(22) \quad \frac{r_{CN}}{r_{NA}} - \frac{r_{CW}}{r_{NA} \ k_A} = \frac{m \ r^2_{NI}}{r_{NA}} - \frac{m \ k_I \ r^2_{NI}}{r_{NA} \ k_A}$$

Multiply Equation (22) by $r_{NA} \ k_A$

$$(23) \quad k_A \ r_{CN} - r_{CW} = m \ k_A \ r^2_{NI} - m \ k_I \ r^2_{NI}$$

Transpose and factor terms.

$$(24) \quad r^2_{NI} \ m \ (k_A - k_I) = k_A \ r_{CN} - r_{CW}$$

Divide by m $(k_A - k_I)$

$$(25)\quad r^2_{NI} = \frac{k_A\, r_{CN} - r_{CW}}{m\,(k_A - k_I)}$$

This is the first of the formulas which we are seeking. It expresses r'_{NI} in terms of the (known) coefficients of correlation found for pairs of the "resultant" phenomena, and of the constants which are to be evaluated.

Transpose terms in Equation (17).

$$(26)\quad r^2_{NA}\, k_A = r_{NW} - k_I\, r^2_{NI}$$

Divide by k_A

$$(27)\quad r^2_{NA} = \frac{r_{NW} - k_I\, r^2_{NI}}{k_A}$$

This is the second formula sought. It expresses r'_{NA} in terms of the (known) coefficient, r_{NW}, of the above mentioned constants, and of r'_{NI}, which has already been evaluated in equation (25). The actual formulas, it will be noted, give the squares of the coefficients instead of the coefficients themselves. The roots are not taken, because it is the squares which are used in computing the final measures of association, the percentage reduction in scatter.

THE VALUES OF THE CONSTANTS

The first constant which must be given a definite value concerns the relative importance of the agricultural factor for changes in the number of colored farmers, and for changes in the number of white farmers. The problem at hand is to determine, from the facts of the southern agricultural situation, the most probable value of this constant. The (migratory) reaction of any group of farmers to the condition of agriculture would depend upon the following factors: a. Their dependence upon particular type of agriculture practiced at the time. (On the one hand, the ability to change their activity when the particular type involved presents unusual difficulties. On the other, their ability through changes in activity to take advantage of unusually profitable conditions in the production of other crops.) b. Their technical competence, and in particular, their contact with new developments in technique which aid in meeting new developments in the agricultural situation. (Their technical resources for meeting new difficulties or taking advantage of new opportunities.) c. Their financial resources. (Again, either for carrying through a period of stress, or for securing the full benefits of favorable conditions.) These several points will be discussed from the standpoint of race differences. The conclusions drawn in the individual cases will then be combined into an estimate of the single constant in which we are interested.

The first point concerns the relative flexibility in the type of activity for the colored and for the white. What differences are found for the two races with respect to the possibility of making adjustments to agricultural conditions through changes in the kind of product raised? While southern agriculture has been organized traditionally about the production of cotton, other crops and farm products are turned out. The colored farmers concentrate upon the production of cotton more than the whites.[1] Does this mean

---

[1] This is shown by the differential proportion of total crop acreage devoted to cotton by the two races. For example, in 20 counties in the Piedmont regions in 1924, the colored farmers devoted 49% of their crop acreage to cotton, while the white farmers devoted only 34%. In other regions the differential is sometimes much greater. It arises in part because, tenure class for tenure class, the colored farmers devote more acreage to cotton (in this same group of counties, the colored croppers devoted 54% of total acreage, while the white croppers devoted only 42%). The differenial also arises in part from the fact that the "lower" forms of tenants, white and colored, tend to devote more acreage to cotton than the "higher" forms. The proportion of "lower" tenants is greater among the colored farmers, and this results in a higher proportion for cotton acreage among the colored farmers as a class.

that the white farmers practice a more diversified form of agriculture than the colored farmers? If so, it would follow that the white farmers are less dependent on the good or bad fortunes of cotton, both because a larger portion of their income comes from other products, and because with great experience in other crops they can more easily shift into different types of production, as the relative prosperity of the different products changes. The differential between the white and the colored farmers, however, appears much less important when the character of the non-cotton crops and products is pointed out. With a few exceptions, diversification in the Cotton Belt is confined to the production of food for the family, and feed for the animals. The development of such cash crops as tobacco, fruits, and dairy products, has been only of local importance.[1] While the production of food and feed crops on the home farm may mean some increases in the real income of the farmer, the fundamental dependence on cotton as the chief source of revenue remains for all classes of farmers. From the standpoint of concentration upon cotton production, then, the following conclusions with respect to the importance of cotton for the two races may be drawn. First, the white farmers were certainly not more dependent on fortunes of cotton than the colored farmers. Second, there is much to be said for the thesis that the dependence upon cotton was approximately the same for the two races. Third, dependence for the colored farmers may be somewhat greater than that for the

[1] It is important for this study to note that diversification in the South is likely to remain of this "secondary" kind. (See H. H. Bennett, *Soils and Agriculture of the Southern States*, 1921, pp. 17-18. *Cf. Year Book,* Department of Agriculture, 1921, p. 343, and C. O. Brannen, *Relation of Land Tenure to Plantation Organization*, Bulletin 1269, Department of Agriculture, 1924, pp. 52-60). While the agricultural factor may change in the future because of progressive adjustments to the boll weevil, it is still likely to be centered about the production of cotton.

whites, and this possibility must be recognized in the subsequent analysis.

A consideration of the other factors enumerated leads us to somewhat the same conclusions. Concerning the technical competence of the two races, it can be said that the colored farmers have less than the white, and further that they are less in touch with new developments, such as new methods of controlling the boll weevil. On the other hand, because of the tenure arrangements which involve close supervision of operations the superior knowledge of the whites benefits the colored farmers. So, with financial resources. While the colored farmers are on the average much lower in the economic scale than their white neighbors, the financial resources of the white landlords form a reserve for the colored tenants as well, both in helping the colored farmer to survive a period of hard times and in allowing him to adopt new and more expensive methods of cultivating his cotton. In both cases, the conclusion may be drawn that the agricultural factor was almost certainly not more important for the white than for the colored farmers, that something like racial equality with respect to the importance of the agricultural factor was very probable, and that the possibility of an appreciably greater importance for colored farmers than for white farmers must be recognized.

In the light of these considerations, the analysis is carried on with two assumptions as to the relative importance of the agricultural factor in the changes in number of white farmers and the colored farmers respectively. It is assumed, first, that the agricultural factor is equally important for both races, and second, that it is twice as important for the colored farmers as for the whites.[1] These two assumptions represent the extremes of the probable facts. The actual

[1] The actual values of k corresponding to those ratios of importance are 1.00 and 0.75. Compare the footnote on page 76.

ratio undoubtedly lies between. Because of the method of analysis employed, a conclusion which holds for both assumptions also holds for any ratio between those contained in them. Such conclusions may be given great weight, even though the exact ratio of importance is not known.

The second undetermined constant in the formulas represents the relative importance of the industrial factor in the changes in number of farmers for the two races. Did the demand, or lack of demand, for industrial labor cause the movement of the white population to as great an extent as the colored? What is the most probable value which may be assigned to the ratio of importance for the two races? What evidence we have concerning this question, evidence from general reports such as those discussed in Chapter V, would indicate that relatively little pressure was brought to bear upon the southern whites during the period being studied, by industrial labor demand. The conclusion drawn from the evidence is considerably strengthened by the general logic of the situation. The War migration of the Negro had opened for him the way from the farm to the factory as it had not been opened before. The Negro himself had realized the possibilities of going into industry. The employer, on the other hand, had recognized the value of the Negro worker, not only because of his respectable record as a worker, but because of his lack both of union organization and union sentiments. The stage was therefore set in the post-war period for the industrial demand for colored labor. It is reasonable to assume that the industrial factor was of little importance for the changes in white farmers during the period. The ratio between the importance of the industrial for the white farmers, and that for the colored farmers is put at zero in the subsequent analysis. It is unfortunately not possible to check this assumption by taking two ratios because of the manner in which k_1 enters into Equations (25) and (27).

It has been found impossible to determine the value of the third constant, m. Furthermore, no substitute equation has been found. It happens, however, that conclusions may be drawn concerning the relative importance of the agricultural and industrial factors, even though the actual value of r_{N1} may not be computed from Equation (24). The meaning of this statement will become clear as the results are presented.

RESULTS OF THE ANALYSIS

One of the geographical divisions discussed in Chapter VI exhibits characteristics which make possible an application of the method of analysis just outlined. The group of counties in the southeastern section of the Cotton Belt shows prevailing decreases in the number of colored farmers from 1919 to 1924, indicating a general (net) movement out of this territory. Further, clear evidence is found that both the agricultural disorganization caused by the newly-arrived boll weevil, and the demand for industrial labor, played substantial roles in this migration. The results of the analysis applied to this group of counties appear in Tables XVII and XVIII.

In Table XVII one finds the degree of association between the changes in number of colored farmers and the agricultural factor. This value has been computed directly from Equation (27), in which the constant m does not appear.[1] Two values have been computed, one for $k_A = 1.00$ and the other for $k_A = 0.75$. Because of the nature of the function expressed in Equation (27), the value of PR would lie between the two values 29% and 41% if the value of k_A lay between the two values chosen. Since there is reason to believe that the two values of k_A represent the limits within

---

[1] Because k_1 is taken equal to zero, the term involving r^2_{N1} (which depends in part on m) drops out.

TABLE XVII

MEASURES OF ASSOCIATIONS

BETWEEN PERCENTAGE CHANGES IN THE NUMBER OF COLORED FARMERS,
1919-1924, AND THE AGRICULTURAL FACTOR

For counties in Georgia and South Carolina, and for two values of k_A

k_A	Number of counties	Percentage reduction in variation (PR)
1.00	72	29%
0.75	72	41%

Source of data: *United States Census of Agriculture.*

TABLE XVIII

UPPER LIMITS FOR MEASURES OF ASSOCIATION

BETWEEN PERCENTAGE CHANGES IN THE NUMBER OF COLORED FARMERS,
1919-1924, AND THE INDUSTRIAL FACTOR

For counties in Georgia and South Carolina, and for two values of k_A

k_A	Number of counties	Percentage reduction in variation (PR)
1.00	72	30%
0.75	72	19%

Source of data: *United States Census of Agriculture.*

which the actual value lay, we may conclude that the actual
PR did lie between 29% and 41%. In Table XVIII there
appears a figure giving the upper limit of the measures of
association for the industrial factor. For while we cannot
compute the actual value of PR, its upper limit is determined by the value of PR for the agricultural factor, because of a fundamental mathematical relation in the theory

of correlation.[1] It is true here again that if k_A actually lay between the two values taken, the upper limit of PR lay between 19% and 30%. As a matter of fact, the actual PR probably had a value considerably below the maximum given. For it would reach that maximum only under the condition that the agricultural and industrial factors explain the changes in number of colored farmers completely, there being no other causes of the migration. We may conclude, therefore, that the agricultural factor was of more importance in the southeastern states than the industrial factor.

It should be emphasized that the results presented in Tables XVII and XVIII rest upon certain assumptions, namely, that the various elements of Equations (4), (5), and (6) are unassociated (that is, A, I, X_N, X_W, and X_C(; that the ratio of importance of the agricultural factor for white and Negro migration (as measured by the corresponding PR's) lay somewhere between one-half and one; and that the industrial factor did not enter appreciably into the migration of whites. Since each of these assumptions is only approximately true, it is the general magnitudes rather than the precise values of the results found in the tables which are of interest. The exigencies of the mathematical method pursued require that our knowledge of the situation be formulated in rigid terms. But elasticity may be reintroduced into the analysis through a broad interpretation of the findings.

It may be noted that this result does not contradict certain other evidence that, taking the Cotton Belt as a whole, the demand for industrial labor was somewhat more important in the migration of the Negro than agricultural conditions. The results of the present chapter have to do with

---

[1] Namely, that the sum of the squares of the net correlation coefficients between a dependent variable and any or all of the independent variables must not be greater than unity.

the reaction of Negro farmers to certain economic conditions. The total importance of the industrial or the agricultural factor, however, depends both upon the reaction of the farmers and the strength of the factor involved. Even though we may generalize from the section studied to the whole Belt with respect to the reaction of farmers, the strength of these factors vary from region to region and the average strength for the whole Belt was presumably different from that in the southeastern states.

CHAPTER V

HISTORICAL SEQUENCES

IN any study of causal relations, the question of sequence of events is of great importance, since the cause must precede the effect, or at the latest coincide with it. Much may be learned, therefore, concerning the causes of a given phenomenon, by noting the conditions which preceded or coincided with it. Did the Negroes move when agricultural conditions warranted it, or did they move when the industrial factor was most influential? To answer such a question, it is necessary to study in detail the whole period from 1919 to 1924, in order to determine the time relationships between the Negro population movements and the changes in agricultural and industrial conditions.

NEGRO MIGRATION, 1919-1924

The principal source of information concerning migratory movements is to be found in the publications of the Federal Reserve Board and of the four Federal Reserve banks in the southern part of the country.[1] These give full reports of economic conditions in general, and agricultural conditions in particular. The information given in the former source is of two kinds, namely, direct references to migratory movements and discussions of the labor supply in the Cotton Belt. Interpreted in the light of the corresponding

[1] These banks are located in Richmond, Atlanta, Dallas and St. Louis. The publications of these banks are entitled *Monthly Review*, and are dated with the day of issue. In the present chapter, however, they are referred to as the Review of a given month, e. g. the Richmond Review for June.

condition of the demand for agricultural workers, this last information furnishes a clue to the shifts in population as between rural and other territory. We shall therefore present the evidence which is given, season by season, for migration during the period. Our object will be primarily to discover when such migrations occurred.

Before the information for the period which we are studying is examined, it should be recalled that during the war activity from 1916 on, a rather considerable number of southern Negroes either migrated to the northern industrial states or went into the urban centers of the South. At the beginning of our period, therefore, there was definitely a condition of labor scarcity. The reports should be judged in the light of that fact.

During the first part of 1919 there seems to have been a slightly more ample supply of labor than in the period before the Armistice. The Richmond Review reports in March: " Labor is more plentiful, but returning soldiers, white and colored, are not inclined to return to farm work." The Atlanta Review reports " still an appreciable shortage of farm labor, though possibly not so acute as formerly reported." Later in the year a somewhat more unfavorable situation with respect to the supply of farm labor in the South obtained. Thus it was stated in the Atlanta Review for July that " all reports indicate a shortage of farm labor which in some instances appears to be acute. In one case it is reported in Alabama that as much as $3.00 a day has been offered for chopping weeds and grass out of cotton." The *Federal Reserve Bulletin* for October says, " there is considerable shortage of labor, and, where obtainable, prices being paid are abnormally high." The St. Louis Review for July reports " a strong demand for competent farm labor in the South," and the Richmond Review for December indicates a scarcity of farm labor.

In the available material, then, there is evidence that the supply of farm labor was somewhat more plentiful in the early part of 1919 than in the later months. Caution should be exercised, however, in interpreting these facts in terms of a considerable return movement of the Negro, either from the North or from the Southern urban centers. We shall see elsewhere that there is some evidence of a decrease in the demand for farm·labor, at least in the early part of 1919, as compared with the demand in 1918. The factor of demobilization of soldiers must also be taken into account. In short, there seems to be little evidence of a continuation of the northward migrations of 1916 and 1917, or of any great movement in the opposite direction.

During the early part of 1920 there were reports throughout the Cotton Belt of a scarcity of labor rather more stringent than that observed in the latter part of 1919. Thus in the Atlanta Review for February it is stated that " the farmer . . . is viewing the coming season with much concern over the farm labor situation. High prices paid in the city and urban industries continue to attract laborers from the country. Much is being done to supplant man power on the farms with horse-power; the purchase of tractors and other farm machinery is heavy." Soon after, the same situation was reported from other sections as well. The Richmond Review of March reports that " available farm labor is so scarce as to make extensive agricultural operations impractical and many large farms are being cut up and sold." The Atlanta Review for the same date also reports that " conditions on the farms are serious as the time approaches for spring work and planting, and unless some relief is had from the acute shortage of farm labor reduced acreages of all crops may result in a continuation of persistent high prices for farm products." The same condition was prevalent in the western part of the Cotton Belt, where "stringent labor shortage is reported from all sections in this district producing cotton." (St. Louis Review for April.) In the Dallas district also, in February, "the labor shortage was and remains the farmer's greatest difficulty and problem, a problem which authorities predict will be still further accentuated in 1920 as a result of the prosperous conditions of last year which enabled so many tenant farmers to rise from tenancy to ownership." In May the same district reports, "While conditions still indicate a large amount of idle farm land in this district this year for lack of man power to cultivate it at wages that can be paid, the shortage has been to some extent offset by the increased use of power implements."

This labor scarcity arose in part, at least, through migration, as indicated in these reports, rather than through an increased demand for agricultural labor. It will be recalled that the February report from Atlanta mentions the high city wages as constituting an attractive force for the country labor. A report from Richmond in April also speaks of the urban movement: "The march from the farms to the cities continues, and the farmers are turning rapidly to machines in an effort to keep their fields under cultivation." In May the Richmond Review is of the opinion that the farm labor scarcity will continue "until wages paid in the cities for unskilled labor fall materially."

A slightly different movement took place at this time in the western part of the Belt. "A heavy exodus of farm workers has occurred in Eastern Texas to the oil fields of Northern Louisiana." On the other hand, there was an influx of "a considerable number of Mexicans who had been attracted by the opportunity to obtain steady work and uninterrupted employment." Possibly this adds weight to the reports of labor scarcity in their significance for the movement of colored labor. For if white labor was increasing in number, the continued labor scarcity indicates that the exodus of colored labor was great enough to counterbalance these white increases. This movement of Mexicans, however, affected only a limited area, and the point is not of far-reaching importance for the Cotton Belt as a whole.

Apparently this acute labor shortage lasted well into the summer of 1920. As late as August the *Federal Reserve Bulletin* reporting for the Atlanta district states that "the labor shortage continues in the rural districts. There appears, it is said, to be no relief from the shortage of farm labor which has existed from the beginning of the war." In the same number of the *Bulletin,* however, it is stated that "in the extreme Southern part of the country a better supply of agricultural labor has resulted from the slackening of industrial production." Later reports indicate an increase in supply of agricultural labor. The Atlanta Review for September says: "Reports indicate that the supply of farm labor shows some improvement, although insufficient and high priced. Mississippi reports denote an adequate supply of labor for harvesting the crops. In Louisiana crops have not suffered from the lack of labor as much as they have been handicapped by its inefficiency and the short hours and high wages." There is also some evidence that the extreme west of the Cotton Belt showed improved conditions somewhat before the eastern section. St. Louis reports as early as July that the "predicted record shortage of labor for harvesting and general agricultural operations in this region has not been verified in anything like the magnitude suggested." In the June issue of the St. Louis Review, it is stated that "farm labor is scarce but less so than elsewhere." Later reports from this district also indicate a sufficient amount of labor. In the Richmond district, on the other hand, reports of labor scarcity continue even up to November, at which time it is reported that "cotton pickers and corn huskers have been scarce and hard to get even at high wages."

The conclusions which are to be drawn with respect to Negro migration during the year 1920 should take account of the fact that a larger amount of cotton was raised than in the previous year. The fact that complaints were of such a vigorous nature during this period does not indicate a wholesale movement from the cotton section, for an increased demand for labor results in labor scarcity, even when the labor supply is constant. But that some movement occurred is to be inferred from the general tenor of the labor supply reports, supplemented by the specific references to such movements which have been noted. In the latter part of the year, with the cotton planted and the labor demand determined, reports of increasing labor abundance may be interpreted in terms of increased number of workers. It is somewhat safer to conclude that there was a movement back into the agricultural districts. The evidence for the first two years of the period seems to warrant the general conclusion that during the intense industrial activity of those two years there was probably some shift to Southern towns and cities and perhaps to the North, followed in the latter part of 1920 by a rather definite readjustment of the labor supply as between the cotton-growing and other lines of activity. This readjustment took place later in the eastern part of the Belt than in the West, although the evidence for this conclusion is somewhat scanty.

The supply of labor, which had been increasing in the latter part of 1920, was even more abundant in the first part of 1921. The Atlanta Review for March says, " Farm labor is reported cheap and increasingly efficient." In April the same Review states: " Farm labor is reported plentiful throughout the district. The supply is better than for several years past." In the Richmond district also we find that by February " enough persons have returned to the rural sections to assure the farmers an ample supply of labor for 1921 operations." In the May number of the Review the same district reports that " farm labor is more plentiful than the demand and wages naturally have been greatly reduced." Dallas reports in March that " Texas farmers . . . are now finding the farm labor supply sufficient and wages settling to a normal level." In May, " an unusually large surplus of farm labor is reported from the rural districts " (Dallas, May, 1921). Similar reports come from the St. Louis district.

Two factors entered into this increase in the relative supply of farm labor. In the first place the demand for such labor was considerably reduced in 1921 because of an actual curtailment of acreage planted to crops and also because the relative amount of farm labor used in the cultivation of the cotton was considerably reduced. " Many farmers and their families are doing their own field work, cultivating only as much land as they are able to manage themselves. As a result of this inability to employ labor several thousands of Georgia's best areas will not be brought under the plow this year." The " growing tendency of farmers to cultivate only such acreages as they are able to take care of without hired help " was rather prevalent throughout the Cotton Belt, both in 1921 and in 1922, a fact of importance in the proper interpretation of the reports concerning labor supply.

There is evidence that a second factor in the increase of labor supply during 1921 was an actual return of laborers from the North to the Southern urban centers and eventually to the agricultural regions. According to the Richmond Review of January " it is reported that on account of decreased industrial activities colored laborers who left the South to work in Northern and Eastern centers are returning, and it is hoped that their return will help the farm

situation." It has been seen that by February the farm labor
situation in·the Richmond district was rather satisfactory
and the Richmond Review attributes this to a small but
sufficient "back-to-the-farm movement." This general situation persisted through the rest of the 1921 season and there
are consistent reports of the ample supply of farm labor
throughout the Cotton Belt for the rest of the year.

The surplus of farm labor which was characteristic of
1921 continued throughout the earlier months of 1922.
Various estimates of the supply and demand made by the
Department of Agriculture and reported in the Atlanta Review for April bear this out. Reports from the Dallas and
St. Louis districts are of the same general tenor. There
still existed a reduced demand resulting from the effort on
the part of farmers to use as little hired labor as possible,
especially in the Atlanta district. "Farmers generally
throughout the district are short of funds to employ labor
and are doing as much farm work as possible themselves,
and are endeavoring to keep expenses down as low as possible." As the season progressed the same general labor
situation prevailed except in certain sections of Georgia in
which, according to the Atlanta Review for June, farm
work made "large demands on the supply of available
labor." The Richmond Review for June reports ample labor
relative to the reduced demand for hired labor. The Western districts also report plentiful farm labor as late as
December, 1922, at which time the St. Louis Review reports that "farm help is plentiful, but farmers in many
localities are refusing to pay the wages asked, and are doing
much of their own work."

At the end of 1922 a new situation arose which is of
special importance in our study. The Review of Richmond
for December makes the following statement concerning
actual migration of the Negro and particularly of the Negro

farmer from that district. " Reports of serious conditions among the tenant farmers of lower and central South Carolina are reaching us. Few tenants have surplus funds [because of the 1922 boll-weevil damage], and are unable to secure work to tide them over; in many instances their landlords are unable to " carry " them through the winter. As a result, many Negroes are leaving the farms for Northern cities. An important effect of the migration is the possible shortage of tenant labor in the cotton plantations next year." The northward movement of the Negro was soon observed in other parts of the Cotton Belt. In March, 1923, the St. Louis Review remarked upon a " heavy movement of farm labor to industrial centers." The same Review reports a month later that a shortage of labor was observed in many counties of the Cotton Belt, the result of " the drain of workers to the industrial centers." The region most affected by this movement, however, continued to be the southeastern states. The Richmond Review of April reports a continuation of the movement in rather large proportions and ventures certain interesting comments upon the character of the movement. " The shortage [of labor] appears to have come about as a result of two developments, one being a general increase in productive, constructive, and industrial activities, the other arises from a rather serious exodus of laborers from the district to the industrial centers of the North and Middle West. The migration has been chiefly made up of farm laborers, who have become discouraged as the result of low prices received for their products in comparison with prices asked for the goods they have to buy or who have been frightened by the ravages of the boll weevil." It is evident here that the term " farm laborer " is being used so as to include " farmers."

By the middle of the summer this movement reached such proportions as to become the object of special study on the part of the Department of Agriculture. The general findings of this study were that the movement was far greater in the southeastern cotton states of Georgia, South Carolina and Alabama than elsewhere. Later a more detailed study on the part of the Department of Labor resulted in about the same conclusion with respect to the geography of the movement. Both in June and July reports from the Richmond district indicated a continuation of the movement Northward. "The migration of colored men from the farms to the Northern and Middle Western industrial centers appears to continue unabated, and Southern employment agencies report the agents for large corporations in industrial centers are exceedingly active. . . . The number leaving North Carolina and Virginia is less than that leaving South Carolina, but is still sufficiently large to cause concern in the agricultural section that depends upon hired labor." (Richmond Review, June, 1923.)

The causes of this movement have been commented upon in the Review: " The migration in North Carolina and Virginia appears to be based upon glowing pictures of supposed conditions awaiting the Nègroes in Northern centers, but in South Carolina many Negroes have left the state because of stern necessity. In the sections of the state which have felt the full ravages of the boll weevil there are hundreds of Negroes who have found it really difficult to get sufficient money or credit to provide for the barest necessities of life, and many of the land owners for whom the Negroes formerly worked are in little better position." The Review goes on to state that large plantations were suffering more from loss of tenant labor than the smaller land owners, largely because of the more personal relations between the landlords and tenants in the latter case. The Richmond Review for July reports a continuation of the movement northward, a movement which involved now, not only colored men but the wives and children of the men who had previously migrated. Reports of a scarcity of labor continued to come from other parts of the Cotton Belt during the months of June and July.

The early fall, however, apparently witnessed a cessation of this movement: " The migration of Negroes to Northern and Eastern industrial centers appears to be slowing down materially and some reports indicate that some of the Negroes who went North several months ago are returning to the South " (Richmond Review, September).

The season of 1924 was apparently not marked by any great movement of colored workers northward. In fact, in the Atlanta district, " reports indicate that quite a number of the colored farmers are returning from the Northern states. (January) Various states in the Atlanta district report a more ample supply of labor during the whole of the 1924 season. Considering the fact that there was no very great reduction in the scale of cotton cultivation during that year, this would seem to indicate at least a partial return of farm laborers from the towns and cities of the South and perhaps even from the Northern industrial states. A rather different situation, however, obtained in the Richmond district. In each of the Reviews for the year there are rather consistent reports of scarce and high-priced labor. The *Federal Reserve Bulletin* of July speaks of " a shortage of labor for cultivating . . . from the Richmond and Atlanta districts, especially in those sections where the smaller farmers have been forced to seek employment in other industries on account of the almost complete failures in other years." Thus in 1924 there occurred a rather definite readjustment of the labor situation which had been created by the 1923 migrations except in the southeastern states of South Carolina and Georgia.

The evidence which has been found concerning the movement of the Negro population during the period from 1919 to 1924 may now be summarized. In the early part of 1919 there appeared to be a rather more abundant labor supply than had obtained during the preceding war years. But this ample supply does not necessarily indicate return from the North, because of a decreased demand for labor, and the demobilization of soldiers. Beginning later in 1919 there is evidence of increased labor shortage. While this was in part due to increased planting of cotton, some north-ward migration occurred as well. There followed, however, conditions of abundant supply of agricultural labor in the South in late 1920 and in 1921 and early 1922, which was due in part to a return from the North.

Up to this point, therefore, two movements of Negro population have been indicated, a northward migration in 1919 and early 1920, followed by a movement in the oppo-site direction. As far as one may judge from the available reports, neither of these movements was of very substantial volume. The second half of the period from 1919 to 1924 witnessed a northward migration of the Negro which ap-parently was of very considerable proportions. Beginning in the early autumn of 1922, the movement continued for approximately a year. In late 1923 it slowed down. The period following the cessation of this chief post-war migra-tion was of relative quiescence as far as the movement of the Negro is concerned, with the possible exception of a slight return from the North in 1924.

Thus it has been possible to find a definite pattern in the timing of movement of the Negro. In semi-tabular form, this pattern is as follows:

First half, 1919, little movement.
Latter half, 1919 and first half, 1920, some drift north-
    ward.

Latter half, 1920, 1921 and first half, 1922, some movement back to the South.

Latter half, 1922 and first half, 1923, pronounced northward migration.

Latter half, 1923, and 1924, slight movement southward.

The year-by-year study of the migration throws light upon the causes of the movement, because of this definite pattern.

THE AGRICULTURAL FACTOR, 1919-1924

The prosperity of the cotton producer is influenced by the price which he gets for his product, and by the difficulties which he may have to meet in making his crop. Information concerning the condition of cotton production, therefore, must include the fluctuations of the price of cotton, on the one hand, and the circumstances affecting the cost of production on the other. During the period under consideration, the chief among these latter circumstances was the damage from the boll weevil. Its importance for our purpose arises both from the fact that it had a very considerable influence upon the cost of producing cotton, and because striking changes in the amount of boll-weevil damage occurred during the period in various parts of the Cotton Belt. For these reasons, a study of variations in cost of production during the period from 1919 to 1924 becomes very largely a study of the amount of damage done by the boll weevil. Secondary factors, such as weather conditions, however, must be considered as well.

Supplementing our information concerning the price of cotton and the difficulties arising from the presence of the boll weevil and other circumstances, there are two kinds of annual statistical data, available by states, which may be used to check the conclusions to which the more direct evidence points. These consist of the average yield of cotton per acre harvested, and the total number of acres harvested.

Variations in the first tend to reflect changes in the conditions under which farmers were raising their cotton. Heavy boll-weevil damage, for example, reduces the amount of cotton obtained per acre of land. Variations in yield, however, arise from causes other than the relative difficulty of production, such as variations in the amount of fertilizer used, or in general changes in the relative intensity of cultivation. They do not, therefore, measure accurately variations in cost of production but they must rather be interpreted in the light of other relevant circumstances. When so interpreted, they serve as a check upon the more direct evidence concerning the boll-weevil damage and other influences upon the general conditions of cotton production.

The second set of figures which serves to check the direct findings concerning the state of cotton production season by season, consists of the number of acres harvested each year. The change in acreage from one season to the next is a fair index of the profitableness of cotton raising in the first of the two seasons; [1] prosperity being indicated by increases in acreage, and hard times by decreases. In contrast to the yield figures, the changes in acreage reflect not only the variations in cost of production, but also variations in price. The acreage figures, therefore, furnish a check upon the conclusions with respect to the condition of cotton production as a whole, including both the effects of price fluctuations and of changes in the cost of production. The problem of interpreting these figures is analogous to that found for the yield per acre, in that they reflect not only the conditions in which we are interested but other factors as well.

[1] Changes in acreage planted rather than in acreage harvested would give a somewhat better picture of the reaction of producers to the condition of cotton in any one season, but such figures are not available.

FARM PRICES OF COTTON

The fortunes of the cotton growers were subject to wide fluctuations during the period from 1919 to 1924 because of changes in the price of cotton.[1] In the first part of the period the price rose rapidly, reaching a record figure of 37½ cents in April 1920. It remained near this maximum from November 1919 to July 1920.[2] This period of high prices was followed by a precipitous decline. In August the price had dropped to 34 cents, in September to 28 cents, in December to 13 cents, and by March 1921 it was under 10 cents, where it remained until July 1921. This fall in price, following upon the extraordinary size of the 1920 crop, together with the general recession of the country as a whole and particularly the restriction of the foreign market, reduced the return far below the cost of production. The situation was so serious throughout the cotton states that the bankers, merchants, and business men generally joined

[1] This price information is to be found in the *Year Book*, Department of Agriculture, 1924, p. 755.

[2] It is worth noting that this rise began in the late spring of 1919 after the 1919 crop had been planted. The statistical analysis of the net changes in acreage from 1919 to 1924, found in previous chapters, becomes more significant because of this fact, for the acreage figures of 1919 are not to be considered as temporarily "inflated" by the temporarily high price. To put it differently, since the price of cotton in both 1919 and 1924 was neither unusually high nor unusually low, changes in acreage between the two years were the reflection of conditions other than fluctuations in price of cotton. This statement would be strictly true if the figures for the acreage planted were being used. The fact that our information concerns the acreage harvested carries with it the possibility that the acreage figures of 1919 were somewhat raised by the high prices of late 1919, since there may have been some increase in the proportion of the planted acreage which was actually harvested. Such increases, however, were probably of minor importance. It should be added that the point is not that prices had no effect on acreage during the period, but that they had no very great influence in determining the acreage in the Census years.

with the farmers to bring about a reduction in the acreage in 1921.[1]

A third phase of the price situation during the years 1919-1924 began with a slight rise in August 1921. By the end of the year the price was around 16 cents, having been up to 18 cents in October. During 1922 the price rose rather consistently, reaching a level of about 24 cents in December. The year 1923 also showed a moderately rising price. The early months of 1924 showed a slight drop, and this downward movement continued throughout the year, the price at the end being 22 cents a pound. It is evident from these facts that fluctuations in the price of cotton during the period studied follow a definite pattern. At the beginning of the year 1919 the price situation was comparatively unfavorable. Then there occurred a rather violent increase in price, the period of high prices lasting from the middle of 1919 to the middle of 1920. This rapid rise was followed by a disastrous decline in late 1920 and in 1921. Beginning in the latter part of 1921, there was once more a season of rising price, and then one of relative stability at a high level, with a slight decline in 1924.

The price of cotton shows comparatively little variation throughout the Cotton Belt, the cotton market being fairly well organized even with respect to the prices paid the actual producer.[2] Fluctuations in the price of cotton, however, did not affect all parts of the Cotton Belt equally, for both methods of cultivation and the cost of production vary considerably from region to region. A series of studies [1] of the cost of production of cotton and general methods of raising it in a number of counties situated throughout the Belt

[1] *Year Book*, Department of Agriculture, 1921, p. 13.

[2] For prices by states see *Year Book*, Department of Agriculture, 1925, p. 962.

[3] See *Year Book*, Department of Agriculture, 1921, pp. 357-63.

indicate wide variations in the use of man labor, mule labor, fertilizer, value of land, and value of equipment. The result is that the cost per pound of producing lint cotton varies from about 30 cents to about 60 cents in different parts of the Cotton Belt. These figures apply for the most part to the year 1919 and are probably representative of the situation which obtained during the fluctuations of the price of cotton in 1920. These studies also reveal the fact that the relative amount of fertilizer used is much greater in South Carolina and Georgia than in the regions west. This finding has an important bearing upon the problem of estimating the rôle played by fluctuations in the price of cotton in the condition of cotton production, as the financial yield of the cotton crop during one season materially affects the amount of money available for the purchase of fertilizer in the following season. For this reason a violent drop in the price of cotton is likely to be felt for a longer period in a region where the use of fertilizer is more important for the profitable growing of cotton. It is to be expected that disastrous price fluctuations, therefore, would be of greater significance in Georgia and South Carolina both because of the higher costs of production and of greater need of fertilizers.[1]

Two conclusions can be drawn as to the effect of price fluctuations upon the condition of cotton growing. The first concerns the timing of such effects. The price of cotton played its chief rôle in the agricultural factor before 1922.

[1] A report in the Review of the Richmond district in early 1922 confirms this conclusion. "The fertilizer is worrying the farmers and comparatively little has been bought. Many farmers have unpaid debts from previous seasons and therefore, are unable to pay costs for fertilizer this year, but fertilizer dealers are charging from $10 to $12 per ton more for goods sold on credit than for goods sold for cash, and in addition are requiring adequate security on the note" (Richmond, April, 1922).

Thereafter, neither very high nor very low prices obtained. The second finding concerns the geographical differences in the effects of price changes. The precipitous decline of 1920 and 1921 undoubtedly proved much more disastrous in the southeastern states of Georgia and South Carolina than elsewhere.

BOLL-WEEVIL DAMAGE

Concerning the amount of boll-weevil damage, 1919-1924, within the area of investigation, there is little exact information. The published figures apply only to states; corresponding information for counties is not available. Furthermore, these figures leave much to be desired in the way of accuracy. They are supposed to indicate the percentage reduction from a " normal " yield which may be attributed to the activities of the boll weevil. Estimates of such a quantity are necessarily rough and the figures which result are significant only in a general way.[1] Large variations in boll-weevil damage for the different states are nevertheless worthy of considerable weight.

Estimates of the damage wrought in the various states by the boll weevil year by year are presented in the table on page 105. It will be noticed that for each state the boll-weevil damage of 1920 was considerably greater than that of 1919, and that in 1921 a further increase is to be observed for all states except Alabama and Mississippi. There was in 1922 a tendency toward geographical differentiation. While in South Carolina the damage increased, and in Georgia the high level already reached in 1921 was maintained, the other states in which boll-weevil damage was an important factor (i. e. excluding North Carolina and Tennessee) showed decreases. In 1923 the situation was reversed, with decreases in the amount of damage in both South Carolina and Georgia, and a considerable increase in Alabama and Missis-

---

[1] See *Alabama Markets Journal*, January 1920, p. 7.

TABLE XIX

PERCENTAGE REDUCTION FROM FULL YIELD PER ACRE, DUE TO BOLL
WEEVIL DAMAGE *—1918-1924

Year	N. C.	S. C.	Ga.	Ala.	Miss.	Tenn.	La.	Ark.	Texas.
1918	..	..	11	12	10	..	10	3	4
1919	..	3	19	29	20	..	29	5	14
1920	..	13	31	36	32	..	26	9	20
1921	4	31	45	32	30	7	35	22	34
1922	12	40	44	26	28	9	25	18	16
1923	13	27	37	33	31	21	23	16	10
1924	7	16	15	12	7	2	5	4	8

* *Year Book*, Department of Agriculture, 1925, p. 957.

sippi. Our conclusion therefore with respect to boll-weevil damage is that the years 1919, 1920 and 1921 were rather disastrous throughout the whole Cotton Belt, that the year 1922 was much worse for the southeastern state of South Carolina and Georgia than for the other states, and that in 1923 Alabama and Mississippi suffered most from the weevil.

These quantitative estimates furnished by the Department of Agriculture may be checked by some general non-quantitative information concerning the ravages of the boll weevil year by year throughout the Cotton Belt. This is found in the current publication of the Federal Reserve Board. The reports do not indicate any particular differentiation among the regions with respect to boll-weevil disaster during the years from 1919 through 1921, which bears out the conclusions concerning the general prevalence of the boll-weevil damage during that period throughout the Cotton Belt. In 1922, however, especially disastrous conditions in Georgia and South Carolina were reported. It will be recalled that the migration [1] of colored farmers reported in

[1] See p. 95.

the latter part of 1922 in South Carolina was accounted for by the extremely disastrous character in the crop year of 1922 in that state. In the *Federal Reserve Bulletin* for November 1922 we find the following comment concerning the condition of the cotton crop: " Deterioration in the condition of the crop is very general throughout the cotton-growing section, but the condition is lowest in Georgia and South Carolina." While the report does not mention specifically boll-weevil damage, it is reasonable to assume that such damage was the most important element in deterioration. Early reports from the Richmond district for the South Carolina cotton section add information which bears out the conclusion that 1922 was a particularly bad year in that state.

COTTON YIELD PER ACRE

The conclusions concerning the fortunes of cotton production which have been drawn from the direct evidence of price fluctuations and difficulties of cotton production may be checked by the study of certain information bearing more indirectly upon the problem. The first type of information to be discussed consists of estimates of cotton yields per acre. These yearly estimates by states are presented in the table on page 107. The figures reflect not only the activities of the boll weevil, but also the weather, the amount of fertilizer used, and other conditions. The same general trend, however, which was found in studying the boll-weevil figures appears also in the table of yields. While the figures fluctuate widely, a recovery from the low point of 1921 appears in all states except South Carolina, where a new low point was reached in the following year. In the case of Georgia, some recovery from the exceeding low point may be observed, although the increase from 1921 to 1922 is very small as compared with the decrease from 1920 to 1921. Since the weather in Georgia was unusually unfavorable in 1921, the

TABLE XX

COTTON YIELD PER ACRE *

Pounds

Year	Va.	N. C.	S. C.	Ga.	Ala.	Miss.	Tenn.	La.	Ark.	Texas
1918....	270	268	250	190	149	187	175	167	158	115
1919....	255	266	240	152	122	160	195	93	155	140
1920....	230	264	254	135	111	140	180	126	194	160
1921....	230	264	140	90	124	148	228	114	160	98
1922....	230	250	123	100	142	157	190	144	173	130
1923....	325	290	187	82	91	91	92	125	98	147
1924....	180	196	160	157	154	176	170	145	169	138

* *Year Book*, Department of Agriculture, 1925, p. 953.

slight increase in yield from 1921 to 1922 is probably the result of more favorable conditions in the second year rather than a reflection of any diminution in the damage of the boll weevil. It will also be noted that according to the yield figures, 1923 was a rather bad year in Alabama and Mississippi, and probably in Arkansas and Louisiana as well. The evidence found in Table XX, therefore, seems to confirm the conclusion already drawn from a study of boll-weevil damage.

COTTON ACREAGE HARVESTED

A final check upon the statements concerning the prosperity of cotton cultivation during the inter-census years may be obtained from the yearly estimates of the number of acres harvested in cotton. Estimates of the total acreage harvested are published annually for the Southern states by the Department of Agriculture. In the table on page 108 these figures are given for ten Southern states for the years 1918 to 1924. In the lower part of the table the data are presented as relatives of the corresponding 1919 figure in order to facilitate the year-by-year comparisons. How

TABLE XXI

Cotton Acreage Harvested, 1918-1924 *

(*Thousand acres*)

Year	Va.	N. C.	S. C.	Ga.	Ala.	Miss.	Tenn.	La.	Ark.	Texas
1918......	44	1,600	3,001	5,341	2,570	3,138	902	1,683	2,991	11,233
1919......	42	1,490	2,835	5,220	2,791	2,848	758	1,527	2,725	10,476
1920......	42	1,587	2,964	4,900	2,858	2,950	840	1,470	2,980	11,898
1921......	34	1,403	2,571	4,172	2,235	2,628	634	1,168	2,382	10,745
1922......	55	1,625	1,912	3,418	2,771	3,014	985	1,140	2,799	11,874
1923......	74	1,679	1,965	3,421	3,079	3,170	1,172	1,405	3,026	14,150
1924......	102	2,005	2,404	3,046	3,055	2,981	996	1,616	3,094	17,175

Cotton Acreage Harvested, 1918-1924

(1919 = 100)

Year	Va.	N. C.	S. C.	Ga.	Ala.	Miss.	Tenn.	La.	Ark.	Texas
1918....	105	107	107	103	92	110	119	110	110	107
1919....	100	100	100	100	100	100	100	100	100	100
1920....	100	107	105	94	102	104	108	96	109	114
1921....	81	94	91	80	80	92	84	77	87	103
1922....	131	109	67	66	99	106	138	75	103	113
1923....	176	113	69	66	110	111	155	92	111	135
1924....	243	135	85	58	110	105	131	106	113	164

* *Year Book*, Department of Agriculture, 1925, p. 952.

closely do these acreage figures reflect the conditions which already have been described? In the first place, it will be noted that in each state, except Alabama, the acreage in 1919 was less than the acreage in 1918, as a result probably of the unfavorable price situation. Moderate increases in acreage were widespread throughout the Cotton Belt from 1919 to 1920, in response to the more satisfactory price of late 1919 and early 1920. These increases were not universal, however. In Virginia there was practically no change in acreage. Decreases occurred in Louisiana and Georgia of four and six per cent respectively. Changes from 1920 to 1921 showed a consistent tendency towards decreases throughout all the states. In only one state, Texas, was the acreage harvested in 1921 greater than the acreage which had been harvested in 1919. The acreage of 1922 was considerably higher than that in 1921 in most of the states of the Cotton Belt. Three states, Louisiana, Georgia, and South Carolina, showed decreases in cotton acreage. The decrease in Louisiana was small, but those in Georgia and South Carolina were of considerable magnitude. The low levels reached in these last two states were also maintained in 1923, while a recovery of some proportion obtained in Louisiana. If we regard the change in acreage from one year to the next as indicating conditions in the first of the two years, it becomes evident that the unprosperous conditions of 1920 were followed by even more unfavorable conditions in 1921 and 1922 in the states of South Carolina and Georgia. A comparison of the 1924 figures with those of 1923 indicates a continued contraction of acreage in Georgia, and a partial recovery in South Carolina. In Alabama, Mississippi, and Arkansas, the figures indicate a relatively unfavorable year for 1923, though it should be noted that in none of these states was there a decrease of the same magnitude as that following the price decline of 1920.

A summary statement of the agricultural factor from 1919 to 1924 runs as follows. The first half of the period was characterized by an unusual increase in the price of cotton, followed immediately by a sharp decline. In the second half of the period, the price stayed at a fairly satisfactory level. The effects of this price disaster, however, probably carried over into the following period, especially in the southeastern states, where high costs and the necessity of using fertilizer render the producers of cotton particularly sensitive to price declines. As for the damage of the boll weevil during the period, the evidence of both quantitative estimates and non-quantitative information points to the following finding. The years 1919, 1920, and 1921 witnessed widespread and increasing damage from the boll weevil. Possibly during this period the southeastern states suffered somewhat more than the other regions. It is certain, in any case, that in 1922, and in the subsequent years, the damage in Georgia and South Carolina was more severe than in other parts of the Cotton Belt. Thus a definite regional pattern appears in the latter part of the period. The other materials analyzed, concerning yields and acreage year by year, do not bear directly upon price fluctuations or boll-weevil and other damage, but the indirect evidence which they furnish adds weight to the conclusions already drawn concerning the two major problems with which this section started, namely, the timing of changes in agricultural conditions and regional differences with respect to this timing.

THE INDUSTRIAL FACTOR, 1919-1924

The second task of the chapter is to trace fluctuations in the demand for industrial labor through the period from 1919 to 1924. For this purpose, it is sufficient to quote year by year Doctor Thorp's general characterization of the state of business together with one or two of his more specific comments.[1] This information follows in semi-tabular form.

1919   Revival; prosperity. (Uncertainty gives way to extraordinary activity, late in spring. Revival in immigration.)

1920   Prosperity; recession; depression. (Great activ-

[1] See Thorp, W. L., *Business Annals*, pp. 143-145.

ity; decline, late spring; stagnation and severe unemployment late in year; large immigration.)

1921 Depression. (Stagnation in many industries; severe unemployment worst, summer; marked reduction in immigration.)

1922 Revival; prosperity. (Gradual but steady recovery; rapid improvement in employment.)

1923 Prosperity; recession. (Activity and record production recede mildly, summer; full employment.)

1924 Mild depression; revival. (Further decline in production to dullness; revived activity, third quarter.)

This summary reveals the following pattern in industrial activity during the period, and therefore in the demand for industrial labor; great activity, 1919 and early 1920; industrial stagnation, and severe unemployment, late 1920 and 1921; activity, 1922 and early 1923. Two periods of labor demand, therefore, were separated by a long period of severe unemployment, that is, of a negative industrial factor. The second period of " positive " labor demand was more important for the southern Negro than the first for the following reasons. Although Thorp characterizes the activity of the first period only as " extraordinary " and " great," a study of various indices of industrial activity shows that the level of activity reached in the two periods was somewhat the same.[1] Moreover, the demand for labor in the first boom was met in considerable part by the demobilized soldiers and the revived immigration, while in the prosperous period 1922 and 1923 the flow of European arrivals had been cut down drastically. The pattern of industrial labor demand as it affected the Negro runs as follows:

[1] See Thorp, *op. cit.*, p. 25.

1919 and early 1920—mild positive demand.

Late 1920, 1921, and early 1922—strong negative demand.

Late 1922 and early 1923—strong positive demand.

Late 1923 and 1924—mild negative demand.

CONCLUSIONS

What light do the historical sequences, revealed by the foregoing study, throw upon the problem of the industrial and agricultural factors in the movement of the Negro? The answer to the question is to be found by comparing time patterns of the migrations, and of the two underlying causes.

The general characteristics of the population movements which occurred during the period from 1919 to 1924 stand out in definite outline. During the first half of the period, there was a minor northward drift, which was followed by a southward movement, also of small proportions. The years 1922 and 1923 witnessed a much larger northward migration.

Both the agricultural and the industrial factors exhibit distinct patterns with respect to timing. From early 1919 to the end of 1921, the difficulties of cotton production were relatively great throughout the Cotton Belt because of the ravages of the boll weevil. While this damage was somewhat counterbalanced at first by high cotton prices, the year 1921, with very low prices added to the weevil devastation, was a particularly bad one in all parts of the cotton region. After 1921, a relative recovery ensued in most parts of the Belt. The price of cotton regained a satisfactory level, and damage from the boll weevil was somewhat reduced. In one section, however, conditions remained depressed. The southeastern states of Georgia and South Carolina continued to suffer from bad times, because the financial reverses of 1921 left a more permanent impress on this section.

In the demand for industrial labor, as it affected the southern Negro, four successive phases may be distinguished. There was one period of relatively light demand for labor in late 1919 and early 1920, a demand which was felt less by the southern Negro because of the large immigration and of the demobilization of soldiers. This was followed by a period of severe urban unemployment in late 1920, 1921, and early 1922, tending to cause the movement of Negroes back to the South. The third, and most important phase consisted of the intense demand for industrial labor of late 1922 and early 1923. The subsequent portion of the period being studied was characterized by mild industrial unemployment.

A comparison of these time patterns aids in estimating the relative importance of the agricultural and industrial factors. The population movements of the Negro may be divided into two successive parts, those before and those after early 1922. The first period witnessed some movement of the Negro northward in late 1919 and early 1920, and some return movement in late 1920 and 1921. Does the agricultural or the industrial factor account for this movement? Industrial labor demand or lack of it, seems to be the important influence at work. For this demand was positive at the time when the Negroes were moving northward in 1919-1920, and negative (that is, discharging rather than taking on workers), when the movement was southward in 1920-1921. That the agricultural factor was of little influence in causing these movements out of and into the South, is shown by the fact that agricultural conditions were relatively good when the Negro was moving northward, and relatively bad when he was returning south. It therefore seems proper to conclude that in the movements of the first years of the period, the industrial factor was more important than the agricultural.

Concerning the much more substantial movement in 1922-1923, the conclusion is somewhat different. The migration began at a time when the industrial demand for labor was picking up and apparently ceased when industrial activity fell off in the latter part of 1923. The industrial factor would therefore seem to explain this movement as well. There is reason to believe, however, that in certain parts of the Belt agricultural conditions played a very important part. It will be recalled that while in most parts of the Cotton Belt relative prosperity returned after the disastrous years 1920 and 1921, in the southeastern states of Georgia and South Carolina agricultural conditions remained very bad. No doubt the agricultural factor was of considerable importance in causing the movement of Negroes out of the southeast in 1922 and 1923. The explanation of the movement which one finds in the reports quoted in the section on the migration attributes much influence to the recent invasion of the boll weevil in this section.[1] Our conclusion, therefore, is that in the major movement of 1922-1923, regional differences appear in the causal situation underlying it. In most parts of the Cotton Belt the industrial factor seems to have been of predominate importance. In the southeast, however, agricultural conditions seem to have been of considerable importance as well.

[1] See p. 95.

CHAPTER VI

The Historical Conclusions Tested

The conclusions reached in the preceding chapter may be tested by an examination of certain information concerning the period before 1919, and by new analysis of the statistical data treated in Chapters II and III.

In the first place, were conditions before the year 1919 such as to lead us to expect the southeastern section of the Cotton Belt to be the principal sufferers from agricultural disorganization during the five-year period following 1919? In order to answer this question it will be necessary to trace the history of the spread of the boll weevil over the Cotton Belt and to study the changes in cotton acreage which occurred between 1909 (the date of the last previous census) and 1919.

The chronology of the spread of the boll weevil over the Cotton Belt gives a good indication of its relative importance in the various parts of the Belt. The disorganization caused by the boll weevil in a community depends considerably upon the length of time during which it has been present. For a season or two after its first appearance, the full effect is usually not felt. Then follows a period of heavy damage and general disorganization of agriculture. Thereafter, the importance of the weevil in the community grows somewhat less. A recovery from the boll-weevil invasion does not involve a diminution of the actual damage inflicted by the pest. Rather what happens is that "after a few years the farmers become accustomed to the weevil injury, learn to distinguish between loss due to the weevil and that attributable to other causes, and are able to reduce weevil injury somewhat by proper farming practices. The first year has been overcome, and comparatively little is said on the subject." [1] In spite of the continued depredations of the pest, its disorganizing influence grows progressively less as time passes.

The boll weevil first entered this country in the southern part of Texas in 1892. In 1903 it reached Louisiana. By 1908 it had covered most of the Cotton Belt west of the Mississippi River,[2] except in northern and central Arkansas, and had entered the southeastern corner of Mississippi. Thus most of the territory west of the Mississippi River had been invaded at least ten years before our period began. Mississippi and most of Alabama had been invaded four or five years before. The spread over most of Georgia took place largely in the season of 1916. South Carolina was covered for the first time in the first year studied, that is, in 1919. In the southeastern section of the Cotton Belt, then, the boll weevil was a comparatively recent invader, and its importance was no doubt much greater in this section than in other parts of the Belt because of this fact. This evidence, therefore, concerning the period preceding 1919 falls in with the general conclusion being tested, that the agricultural factor had much more important influence on the migration of the southern Negro in the southeastern section of the Belt than in other parts.

A study of changes in cotton acreage during the period from 1909 to 1919 reveals a geographic distribution such as one might expect from the history of the boll-weevil invasion which has just been traced. These changes are pre-

[1] *Farm Bulletin 1329*, United States Department of Agriculture, p. 4.

[2] Outside of the "new" Cotton Belt recently opened up in western Texas and Oklahoma.

sented in Plate IV. The increases in acreage west of the
Mississippi River point to the conclusion that in this region
the boll weevil as an acute problem had been taken care of
quite completely before 1919, and that any further changes
in the scale of cotton production after 1919 were brought
about by conditions other than the infestation of this pest.
The effect of the boll weevil in the Mid-Belt section, i. e., in
Mississippi and Alabama, is strikingly evident in the widespread decreases from 1909 to 1919. In Georgia and South
Carolina the diversity of conditions with respect to cotton
acreage changes indicates that the full effect of the boll
weevil had not been felt in 1919.

It is possible to test in still another way the thesis that in
the southeastern states the agricultural factor had an important influence upon the northward movement of the Negro,
while in other parts of the Belt the industrial demand for
labor was the predominant cause of the movement. This
new method of studying the problem consists of an examination, for various geographic divisions, of the associations
between changes in cotton acreage on the one hand, and
changes in the number of colored farmers and of white
farmers, respectively, on the other. For if the relative importance of the agricultural and industrial factors varied
from region to region, this fact should be reflected in the
relative closeness of the two associations mentioned.

In the first lines of Tables XXII and XXIII there are
given the two measures of association for cotton acreage and
colored farmers, and for cotton acreage and white farmers,
in the southeastern states of Georgia and South Carolina.
Do these measures confirm the thesis that in this territory the
movement of the Negro was due to both agricultural and industrial factors? We may assume that the association for
colored farmers reflects the operation of both agricultural
and industrial factors, while that for the whites reflects the

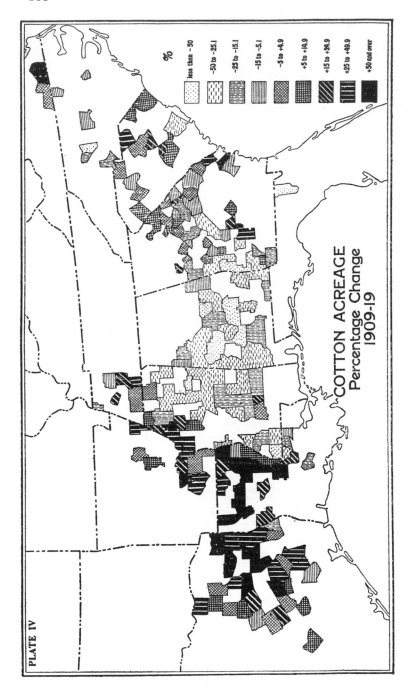

COTTON ACREAGE
Percentage Change
1909-19

%

less than – 50
–50 to –25.1
–25 to –15.1
–15 to –5.1
–5 to +4.9
+5 to +14.9
+15 to +24.9
+25 to +49.9
+50 and over

PLATE IV

TABLE XXII

MEASURES OF ASSOCIATION

BETWEEN PERCENTAGE CHANGES IN THE NUMBER OF COLORED FARMERS,
AND PERCENTAGE CHANGES IN COTTON ACREAGE, 1919-1924

For five groups of counties selected on basis of location

Group	Number of counties	Percentage reduction in variation (PR)
1. Southeastern states	72	37%
2. Counties outside southeastern states with decreasing cotton acreage......	57	10%
3. Mid-Belt region	69	11%
4. Mississippi River Valley	34	20%
5. Texas.	25	4%

Source of data: *United States Census of Agriculture.*

* Not significant in the probability sense.

operation of the agricultural factor only. Under these conditions one would expect the association for colored farmers to be appreciably greater than the association for white farmers. Such is the case, as is shown by the figures in the tables. The colored-cotton association is measured by a reduction of 37 % while that of the white farmers is measured by only 10%.

Does this evidence also sustain the conclusion as to the relatively slight importance of the agricultural factor in other parts of the Cotton Belt? The counties outside the southeastern states which decreased in cotton acreage have been grouped together and are represented in the second line of the tables. It will be seen that the association for colored farmers is moderately close, but there is no appreciable degree of association for white farmers. Apparently, the association for colored farmers reflects the operation of the industrial factor, while the lack of association for the white

TABLE XXIII

Measures of Association

BETWEEN PERCENTAGE CHANGES IN THE NUMBER OF WHITE FARMERS,
AND PERCENTAGE CHANGES IN COTTON ACREAGE, 1919-1924

For five groups of counties selected on basis of location

Group	Number of coun	Percentage reduction in variation (PR)
1. Southeastern states	72	10%
2. Counties outside southeastern states with decreasing cotton acreage......	57	3%
3. Mid-Belt region	69	14%†
4. Mississippi River Valley	34	2%
5. Texas	25	(—) 1%

Source of data: *United States Census of Agriculture.*

* Not significant in the probability sense.

† The difference between the two measures for the Mid-Belt is not significant.

farmers indicates that the factor that would influence them, the agricultural, was of relatively little importance. Thus the agricultural factor was important only in the southeastern states.

In order to test further the causal thesis which is being discussed, the region west of Georgia has been split up into three subdivisions. The first of these consists of the Mid-Belt states of Alabama and Mississippi. The basis for this division is found in the history of the period previous to 1919. Both the cotton acreage changes from 1909 to 1919 and the history of the weevil invasion indicated that in 1919 the full effects of the invasion were being felt in the Mid-Belt region. Thus this region might be expected to show definite recovery from the weevil during the period from 1919 to 1924.

In so far as agricultural recovery took place in the Mid-Belt section, the changes shown in Plate II, p. 27, indicate that such recovery was definitely localized, for counties with increasing cotton acreage are intermingled with those showing decreases. The possibility arises that a considerable part of the population movement in the Mid-Belt region consisted of local migration occasioned by the differential prosperity of cotton growing in the various parts of this region. If this is the case, one would expect the white farmers and the colored farmers to be about equally affected by these agricultural conditions. The measures bear out this expectation, for the associations for white and for colored farmers are equally close,[1] as shown in the third line of the tables.

The question arises whether this result, indicating the operation of the agricultural factor, is in contradiction with the general finding that in the territory west of Georgia the industrial factor seemed to be of chief importance in the northward movement of the Negro. The immediate answer is that we are here dealing with a different problem. Instead of studying the counties with decreasing cotton acreage, that is, counties in which the balance of economic forces may be said to be unfavorable to the county in question, we are now dealing with all counties. Thus there is no conflict between the two results. But this leaves open the relation of this new result to the general causal hypothesis being tested. This relation follows. Population movements in the Mid-Belt were apparently to a considerable extent local in nature. In these local movements, the differential recovery of agriculture, as well as possibly further depression, played a substantial rôle. But such northward migra-

---

[1] As a matter of fact, the association for white farmers is somewhat closer than that for colored farmers. But the difference between them is too small to be significant in the probability sense. In other words, the closer association for white farmers arises merely by chance.

tion as occurred, presumably was caused by industrial labor demand rather than by the push of agricultural disorganization. To put the matter differently, the evidence that local migrations in the Mid-Belt region arose apparently from agricultural causes does not affect the conclusion that northward migration from the territory west of Georgia was the result of industrial labor demand rather than agricultural conditions. When the decreasing counties of the Mid-Belt region were grouped with the other decreasing counties west of Georgia, the influence of the industrial factor appeared. But when the decreasing counties of the Mid-Belt region were grouped with the increasing counties of the same region, the influence of the differential agricultural prosperity of the two classes of counties appeared.

A further division of the territory west of Georgia has been made. The counties lying in the Mississippi River Valley show rather more consistent decreases both in the number of colored farmers and in cotton acreage than those in the regions either on the east or on the west. These decreases suggest a wholesale movement of the colored population out of the territory.

Because the boll weevil had been present in this region for many years, one would expect this exodus to arise more from the industrial rather than from the agricultural factor. That such was the case is indicated by the information presented in the fifth line of the tables. The associations for white farmers,[1] which would reflect the operation of the

[1] In the case of the relation between changes in the number of white farmers and changes in cotton acreage the following difficulty presents itself. In the Mississippi River Valley there are certain counties which show relatively large increases in the number of white farmers, because of the introduction of foreign white tenants. This introduces an element of instability into the distribution in the sense that the value of the measures computed is rather markedly affected by these few cases. The rest of the distribution, however, indicates no relationship between changes

agricultural factor, is negligible, while the association for colored farmers is relatively close.

In this territory a few counties increased in number of colored farmers, or in cotton acreage. These increases are small, however, for the most part, and do not affect the relative closeness of the two associations. As a matter of fact, small increases in the number of colored farmers may be a reflection of industrial labor demand, for under conditions of potential or actual labor scarcity a large shift from wage organization to tenant organization may be made in order to achieve a more stable labor supply. Such a shift on any large scale, however, is possible and effective only under special conditions such as the presence of a number of capable wage earners at the beginning of the period. No doubt such shifts occurred in all counties where labor scarcity was felt. It may very well be, however, that in these few counties the effects of such shifts were much more pronounced. Thus the industrial demand was apparently a predominant factor in this region.

The counties of Texas are represented in the last line of the tables. In this region increases in cotton acreage were apparently not related to a significant degree with either changes in the number of white farmers or changes in the number of colored farmers. The increases in cotton acreage probably reflect a shifting from other forms of activity to the raising of cotton and also the expansion of the scale of operation on individual forms, such expansion being much more feasible in this region than in other parts of the Cotton Belt.[1] Neither of these phenomena would be accompanied

in acreage and changes in the number of white farmers and in the number of colored farmers, and therefore the presence of these outlying cases does not affect the conclusion as to the negligible association for white farmers.

[1] Brannen, *op. cit.*, pp. 83, 84.

by large changes in the amount of labor performed and therefore might be expected to show little relation to the changes in the number of farmers. The changes which occurred in the number of farmers may reflect changes of status more than in other parts of the Belt.

The importance of the conclusions reached in this chapter is very great, for it not only adds weight to the general result of the statistical analysis, namely, that in the post-war movement of the Negro into industry the demand for industrial labor was more influential than agricultural conditions, but it indicates that agricultural conditions will have even less to do with such migrations in the future. For the agricultural factor was important only in the region where its force was most likely to decrease.

CHAPTER VII

THE AGRICULTURAL VS. THE INDUSTRIAL FACTOR

THE foregoing pages have been devoted to a detailed investigation of the economic factors in Negro migration, as between North and South, during the five years from 1919 to 1924. For reasons which have been stated before,[1] this relatively short period constitutes the only available " sample " of Negro population movement of which a thorough analysis can be made. The study of this limited period is of considerable significance. From the standpoint of further research, it has yielded two important contributions, one consisting of certain methodological developments, and the other consisting of certain questions concerning the economic condition of the southern Negro which the investigation raises and to which our findings will aid in obtaining an answer. Furthermore, the conclusions of the investigation have a distinct bearing upon the broader aspects of Negro migration. They help to explain developments since 1924, and to reveal the prospects of Negro migration in the future.

The methodological developments which will be of use in further research result from the necessity of meeting the peculiar difficulties presented in the statistical analysis of the problem. These obstacles arose from the fact that the underlying agricultural and industrial factors were not directly measurable, their operation being revealed through three phenomena into which they entered, namely, Negro migra-

1 See pp. 16-17.

tion, white migration, and changes in the amount of cotton cultivated. The measures of association among these phenomena constitute the only available statistical clue to the action of the agricultural and industrial factors. By manipulation of this indirect evidence the underlying factors have been studied. The methodological contribution of the investigation consists of the specific means by which these indirect data have been exploited.

The analysis of the data—the various measures of association—has been of two distinct types. In the first place, extensive comparisons have been made. The different associations between the several pairs of variables have been compared, and variations of each association in different groups of counties studied. The reason for this procedure is that in the various associations for the same group of counties, and in the same association for different groups, the two underlying factors apparently entered in differential degrees. Because of this fact the comparisons disclose the underlying causal situation. The interesting feature of this part of the analysis lies in the study of relationship, not from the standpoint of the variables immediately involved, but from that of other variables which give rise to the observed association.

The fundamental logic of the foregoing analysis—that of studying underlying forces through an examination of certain associations into which they enter—is carried further in the mathematical method (as contrasting with the strictly statistical) pursued in the second part of the investigation (Chapter IV). Here the available data are made to yield the actual measure of association between the agricultural factor and Negro migration, in spite of the fact that no index of the agricultural factor is available. From this estimated measure, a maximum value for the degree of association between the industrial factor and Negro migration has been found. Thus results have been gained approximating those which direct measures of the underlying factors would have yielded.

These results are possible because of the analytical power of the mathematical method. Essentially this method consists of a formulation in mathematical symbols of what may be broadly termed the theory underlying a given situation—in this instance, the relationships obtaining among the two factors on one hand, and the three " resultant " phenomena on the other. Such a symbolic formulation renders available the powerful technique of mathematical manipulation, bringing to light the implicit quantitative relations of the data. This allows us to exploit the data much more fully than would the ordinary statistical procedure. The success of the method in the present investigation furnishes evidence of a wider applicability than it now has.[1] A further development of the technique employed in Chapter IV appears to hold considerable possibilities of yielding interesting results. It should be noted that the method is not one of " refinement " of results in the sense that the current " corrections " (e. g. that for attenuation) are. The aim is not for greater precision of values. The method does not carry with it the emphasis on exactitude which is so often completely unjustified by the inaccuracy of the original data. The purpose of the mathematical method is to gain results which could otherwise not be obtained at all. As a general method by which statistical data may be further exploited, the mathematical formulation of relationships may prove to be the most fertile field of statistical analysis.

The investigation has not only resulted in certain methodological innovations which are likely to be of further use, but it has also prepared the way for a study of certain phases

[1] Compare the price analysis of Professor Henry L. Moore and the " rational " secular trend analysis of Doctor Simon Kuznets.

of the economic life of the southern Negro. How far was the position of the Negro, who remained in agriculture after the migrations which have been studied, affected by these far-reaching changes which occurred during the period from 1919 to 1924? The effects of such migrations would presumably depend to a considerable extent upon the forces underlying them—the forces which have been the object of study in the present investigation. A fruitful line of research would seem to be a study of the Negro in agriculture in 1924 as compared with his position in previous years, such a study to take account of the regional differences which have been discovered in the forces operating during the period immediately preceding 1924. For this purpose, the unusually detailed information concerning the Negro in agriculture, contained in the 1924 Census of Agriculture and collected immediately after the extensive migration of 1922 and 1923, is available. The 1924 census figures are soon to be supplemented but not surplanted by the census data for the year 1929. These figures are significant both because of their recency and because of the fact that they have been collected after a long period of a less spectacular development in the Cotton Belt. They will serve, therefore, to check conclusions obtained from a study of the 1924 figures, as well as to reveal developments since 1924. In terms of the general problem which has been discussed in this essay, namely, the place of the Negro in the labor supply of the country, such a study would be significant in disclosing more fully the nature and extent of the pressure exerted by southern agricultural conditions toward a further entrance of the Negro into the industrial life of the country.

Aside from the contributions of the investigation to further research, how far may our conclusions be regarded as applying to the period since 1924? What light do they throw upon the prospects of Negro migration in the future?

What is their more general significance in the economic life of the country and in that of the Negro in particular? Before the relevance of the study to this broader aspect of the problem of Negro migration can be discussed, it is necessary to summarize the conclusions which have been drawn for the period from 1919 to 1924. Was the agricultural or the industrial factor of more importance in the movement of the Negro during this period? The answer afforded by the various methods of analysis which have just been mentioned may be stated as follows.

1. Taking the Cotton Belt as a whole, both the demand for industrial labor and the disorganization of southern agriculture were important in the movement of the Negro. The industrial factor, however, exerted a somewhat greater influence than did the agricultural.

2. In the states of South Carolina and Georgia, in which the boll weevil was a recent invader, the agricultural factor was of much greater importance than elsewhere in the Cotton Belt.

3. In this southeastern section, in which both factors were operative, the Negro was apparently somewhat more susceptible to agricultural than to industrial influences. Insofar as the behavior of the southeastern Negro may be taken as typical of that of the southern Negro in general, this would indicate that the predominance of the industrial factor in the movement from the Cotton Belt as a whole, arose from the greater strength of the industrial labor demand as compared with the agricultural factor rather than from the greater responsiveness of the Negro to industrial demand.

4. In the Mississippi River Valley, the pull of industrial labor demand was by far the more important influence upon the migration of colored workers. The agricultural factor was apparently negligible.

In brief, the investigation reveals that the intensity of the demand for industrial labor was so great as to make it the predominant factor in the movement of the Negro. Furthermore, it indicates that during the period from 1919 to 1924 the agricultural factor was most potent in the region where it was likely to decline in strength after 1924, as the advent of the boll weevil receded into the past, and the " psychological " component of the factor diminished in intensity.

The problem of generalizing from these conclusions reduces itself to a discussion of the question whether the underlying forces which operated in the period investigated have continued and will continue to operate in somewhat the same manner, and whether new forces have come in or are likely to appear in the future. What, in other words, are the current and prospective developments in southern agriculture and in the industrial demand for Negro labor which may influence the flow of Negroes as between South and North?

With respect to the agricultural factor, it has already been noted that material changes have occurred since 1924. Whereas the recency of the boll-weevil invasion was shown to be a very important element in the repulsive force of agricultural disorganization during the period studied, there are no longer any regions occupied by the Negro which face the devastating experience of meeting this pest for the first time. Thus the powerful " psychological " effects of the newly-arrived boll weevil will not be a factor in Negro migration in the future. But other agricultural conditions may act as a strong stimulus to the movement of Negroes. For example, the prospective continuance of low cotton prices, and the probable mechanization of cotton growing both are likely to put great economic pressure on the colored farmer. During the years from 1919 to 1924, the low-priced period which did occur was short-lived, and was also characterized by a spectacular lack of opportunities in industrial fields. The fact that the nine-cent cotton of 1921, accompanied as it was by widespread urban unemployment, did not cause a large exodus of colored agricultural workers does not rule out the possible influence of low prices on migration, particularly when they are of long duration.

The chances are good that in the future the influence of cotton prices on the movement of southern Negroes will be strong. The present disorganized state of the cotton market is well known, and the prospects of a recovery are none too bright. But even though the price of cotton in the future attains a level which will compensate adequately the majority of cotton producers, the Negro cultivator will still be in jeopardy of virtual extinction. For prices which will allow the producers in the newer low-cost areas of western Texas and Oklahoma to operate profitably may be very inadequate for those in the older cotton states, in which the Negro chiefly resides. Furthermore, the imminent introduction of a mechanical cotton picker holds the possibility of a complete elimination of the traditional tenant farmer.[1] The consequences of these developments may take somewhat longer to appear and may be less spectacular than those of the weevil invasion. But in the long run they may reinforce the labor demand of the industrialists even more effectively than the weevil has done in the past.

The study has shown that the recent entrance of the Negro into industry was by no means entirely dependent upon the peculiar agricultural situation which obtained in the South during and after the World War. The industrial demand for labor was of itself a potent force in drawing labor even out of those sections of the Cotton Belt in which the agricultural conditions were relatively favorable. Ap-

---

[1] *Cf*. Vance, R. B., *Human Factors in Cotton Culture*, pp. 318-19.

parently the southern Negro constitutes a fairly "easily accessible source of supply" upon which industry can draw regardless of the state of agriculture in the Cotton Belt. Since 1924, the pressure of industrial labor demand has been felt by the southern Negro to far less an extent than during the two years preceding 1924. Industry has been served through other sources, and the Negroes who entered industry found it impossible to maintain their position in the face of competition even before the current period of unemployment began. This does not mean, however, that the Negro has been eliminated as a potential source of expanded labor forces, or that the employers will never again make use of the effective recruiting technique which was utilized in 1922 and 1923, and which proved its worth at the time. The intensity of the industrial factor has diminished in recent years; but with a continued policy of restricted immigration and the inevitable recovery and further advance from the present low levels of industrial activity, circumstances may well shape themselves so as to induce the buyers in the labor market to search out the supply of material quite as thoroughly and effectively as they have done in the past.

It may be concluded, then, that while the powerful economic forces, which in the past have caused the Negro to leave the southern farms and enter the factories and other urban employment, may for the moment be held somewhat in abeyance, the prospect is that in the future Negro migration will continue to arise from the differential economic status of city and country life. Fortunately or otherwise, the industrialization of the colored man seems destined to go on. The importance of this fact for the Negro is difficult to over-emphasize. The economic salvation of the race, in so far as one may be discerned, lies in an adjustment of its members to the status of industrial wage-earners. That adjustment is not a mere matter of learning to perform the simple tasks which modern industry sets for its workers. It is a matter of achieving a satisfactory position in American economic life, and that process has important social and political ramifications. For the white worker, the competition of the colored man is not to be judged merely by the numbers involved. The introduction of racial antagonism into industrial fields endangers for all labor the material benefits which result from the existence of an integrated body of workers. The economic forces which have been studied in this essay may well become predominant influences upon the economic well-being of the common American, white and black.

SELECTED BIBLIOGRAPHY

Baker, Oliver E., "Agricultural Regions of North America," Part I, *Economic Geography*, October, 1926.

——, "Agricultural Regions of North America," Part II, "The South," *Economic Geography*, January, 1927.

Banks, E. M., *Economics of Land Tenure in Georgia*, Columbia University Press, New York, 1905.

Bennett, H. H., *Soils and Agriculture of the Southern States*, New York, 1921.

Bizzell, W. B., *Farm Tenantry in the United States*, College Station, Texas, 1921.

Boeger, E. A., and Goldenweiser, E. A., *Tenant System of Farming in Yazoo-Mississippi Delta*, Bulletin No. 377, Department of Agriculture, 1916.

Brannen, C. O., *Relation of Land Tenure to Plantation Organization*, Bulletin No. 1269, Department of Agriculture, 1924.

Brawley, Benjamin G., *Short History of the American Negro*, New York, 1919, 280 pp.

——, *Social History of the American Negro*, New York, 1921, 420 pp.

Brooks, Robert Preston, *The Agrarian Revolution in Georgia, 1865-1912*, Madison, Wisconsin, 1914.

Coman, Katherine, "The Negro as Peasant Farmer," *Publications of the American Statistical Association*, vol. ix, 1904.

Dixon, H. M., and Hawthorne, H. W., *An Economic Study of Farming in Sumter County, Georgia*, Bulletin No. 492, Department of Agriculture, 1917.

Du Bois, W. E. B.; *Negro Landholders in Georgia*, U. S. Department of Labor, Bulletin No. 35.

Edwards, Thomas J., "The Tenant System and Some Changes Since Emancipation," *Annals of the American Academy*, xlix, 38-46.

Engberg, R. G., *Industrial Prosperity and the Farmer*, Institute of Economics, New York, 1927.

Goldenweiser, E. A., and Truesdell, Leon, *Farm Tenancy in the United States*, Census Bureau, 1920.

Gray, L. C., *et al.*, "Farm Ownership and Tenancy," *Year Book*, Department of Agriculture, 1923, pp. 507-600.

Gray, Lewis, "Southern Agriculture, Plantation System and the Negro Problem," *Annals of the American Academy,* xl, 90-99.

Harper, Roland M., "Rural Standards of Living in the South," *Social Forces,* II, Nos. 1, 2, 1923.

Harris, Abram, "Negro Migration to the North," *Current History Magazine of the New York Times,* vol. 20, pp. 921-5, September, 1924.

Hibbard, B. H., "Tenancy in the Southern States," *Quarterly Journal of Economics,* xxvii, 482-96.

Hubbard, W. H., *Cotton and the Cotton Market,* New York, 1927.

Hunter, W. D., and Coad, B. R., *The Boll Weevil Problem,* Farmers' Bulletin No. 1329, Department of Agriculture, 1923.

Johnson, Guy B., "Negro Migration and Its Consequences," *Journal of Social Forces,* vol. 2, pp. 404-8, March, 1924.

Johnson, W. H., *Cotton and Its Production,* London, 1926.

Kennedy, L. V., *The Negro Peasant Turns Cityward,* Columbia University Press, New York, 1930.

Lovall, R. H., *et al., Negro Migration in 1916-1917,* Department of Labor, Division of Negro Economics, 1919.

Phillips, Ulrich B., "Decadence of the Plantation," *Annals of the American Academy,* xxxv (1910), 37.

Sanders, J. T., *Farm Ownership and Tenancy in the Black Prairie of Texas,* Bulletin No. 1068, Department of Agriculture, 1922.

Scott, Emmett J., *Negro Migration During the War,* New York, 1920.

Smith, J. Russell, *North America,* New York, 1925.

Spero, Sterling and Harris, Abram, *The Black Worker,* Columbia University Press, 1931.

Stone, A. H., "The Cotton Factorage System for Southern States," *American Historical Review,* April, 1915.

Turner, H. A., "The Share Renting of Farms in the United States," *International Review of Agricultural Economics,* October-December, 1923.

Vance, Rupert B., *Human Factors in Cotton Culture,* University of North Carolina Press, Chapel Hill, 1929.

Wesley, Charles H., *Negro Labor in the United States,* Vanguard Press, New York, 1927.

Woofter, T. J., Jr., *Negro Migration,* New York, 1920.

APPENDIX A

SELECTION OF THE COUNTIES

The following criteria were used to select the 238 counties analyzed in the statistical part of the investigation.

1. No changes in boundary from 1909 to 1924. (The earlier date was chosen because the study grew out of a study of the decade from 1909 to 1919.)
2. Rural in 1920.
3. At least 100 colored tenants and at least 100 white tenants in 1919.
4. At least 1000 acres of cotton harvested in 1919.
5. Geographic limitations as indicated on the Key Map.
6. To the group of counties selected according to the above criteria a few were added in order to make possible certain comparisons with a study made in 1909. (Of these one was urban in 1920, 8 lay in the Coastal Flatwoods, a region which was not included in the original study, and the rest changed boundaries from 1909 to 1919.)

APPENDIX B

LIST OF COUNTIES ARRANGED ACCORDING TO MAP NUMBERS

ALABAMA

1. Lamar	16. Autauga
2. Fayette	17. Elmore
3. Pickens	18. Chotaw
4. Tuscaloosa	19. Wilcox
5. Randolph	20. Lowndes
6. Bibb	21. Montgomery
7. Chilton	22. Washington
8. Coosa	23. Clarke
9. Tallapoosa	24. Monroe
10. Chambers	25. Connecuh
11. Sumter	26. Crenshaw
12. Greene	27. Barbour
13. Hale	28. Henry
14. Perry	29. Geneva
15. Dallas	30. Houston

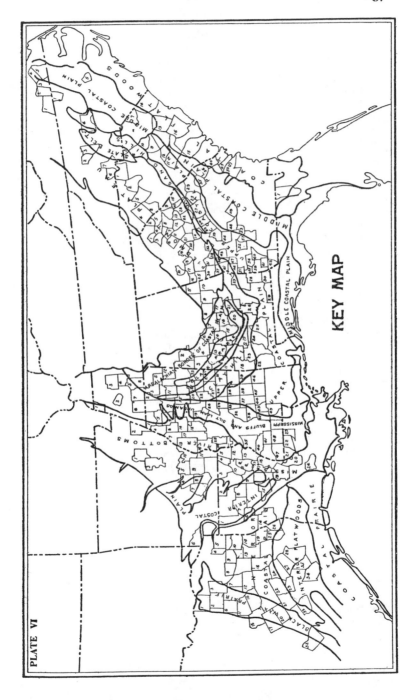

PLATE VI

KEY MAP

ARKANSAS

1. Woodruff
2. Crittenden
3. Prairie
4. Cleveland
5. Lincoln
6. Little River
7. Calhoun
8. Bradley
9. Drew
10. Desha
11. Chocot

FLORIDA

1. Columbia

GEORGIA

1. Banks
2. Hart
3. Jackson
4. Madison
5. Elbert
6. Walton
7. Oconee
8. Oglethorpe
9. Lincoln
10. Douglas
11. Morgan
12. Greene
13. Taliaferro
14. McDuffee
15. Columbia
16. Heard
17. Cowe
18. Fayette
19. Henry
20. Butts
21. Jasper
22. Hancock
23. Warren
24. Glascock
25. Troup
26. Jones
27. Washington
28. Jefferson
29. Burke
30. Harris
31. Talbot
32. Crawford
33. Twiggs
34. Wilkinson
35. Jenkins
36. Screven
37. Muscogee
38. Taylor
40. Effingham
41. Chattahoochie
42. Marion
43. Schley
44. Dooley
45. Bryan
46. Stewart
47. Webster
48. Wilcox
49. Telfair
50. Long and Liberty
51. Quitman
52. Lee
53. Turner
54. Jeff Davis
55. Clay
56. Calhoun
57. Worth
58. McIntosh
59. Early
60. Baker
61. Miller
62. Decatur and Seminole
63. Camden

LOUISIANA

1. Bossier
2. Union
3. Morehouse
4. West Carroll
5. East Carroll
6. Red River
7. Bienville
8. Jackson
9. Caldwell
10. Richland
11. Franklin
12. Madison
13. Tensas

14. Sabine
15. Grant
16. La Salle
17. Catahoula
18. Concordia
19. Avoyelles
20. Point Coupee
21. West Feleciana
22. East Feliciana
23. St. Helena
24. St. Martin
25. West Baton Rouge
26. Livingston

MISSISSIPPI

1. DeSota
2. Benton
3. Tippah
4. Tunica
5. Tate
6. Prentiss
7. Coahoma
8. Quitman
9. Panola
10. Lafayette
11. Pontotoc
12. Itawamba
13. Bolivar
14. Tallahatchie
15. Calhoun
16. Washington
17. Sunflower
18. Leflore
19. Carroll
20. Webster
21. Clay
22. Chotaw
23. Lowndes
24. Issaqueha
25. Sharkey
26. Attala

27. Winston
28. Noxubee
29. Leake
30. Neshoba
31. Kemper
32. Rankin
33. Scott
34. Newton
35. Claiborne
36. Simpson
37. Smith
38. Jasper
39. Clarke
40. Jefferson
41. Franklin
42. Lawrence
43. Jeff Davis
44. Covington
45. Jones
46. Wayne
47. Wilkinson
48. Amite
49. Marion
50. Lamar
51. Greene

140

APPENDIX B

NORTH CAROLINA

1. Warren
2. Davie
3. Davidson
4. Chatham

5. Greene
6. Gaston
7. Mechlinburg

SOUTH CAROLINA

1. York
2. Union
3. Chesterfield
4. Anderson
5. Laurens
6. Kershaw
7. Dillon

8. Abbeville
10. Lee
11. Orangeburg
12. Calhoun
14. Horry
15. Colleton

TENNESSEE

1. Lake
2. Crockett
3. Carroll
4. Henderson

5. Chester
6. Fayette
7. Hardeman
8. McNairy

TEXAS

1. Grayson
2. Collin
3. Hunt
4. Morris
5. Cass
6. Dallas
7. Van Zandt
8. Wood
9. Upshur
10. Harrison
11. Ellis
12. Henderson
13. Rusk
14. Panola
15. Hill
16. Navarro
18. Cherokee

19. Shelby
20. Falls
21. Robertson
22. Leon
23. Madison
24. Houston
25. San Augustine
26. Sabine
27. Trinity
28. Polk
29. Tyler
30. Jasper
31. Newton
32. Travis
33. Burleson
34. Montgomery
35. San Jacinto

VIRGINIA

1. Mecklinburg
2. Brunswick
3. Greenville

4. Sussex
5. Southampton

APPENDIX C

List of counties, by state and map number, eliminates from the total group of counties, because of "instability". See p. 46.

North Carolina, 1, 2, 3, 4, 5, 6, 7
Tennessee, 1
Texas, 15, 25, 26, 27, 28, 32, 33
Virginia, 1, 2, 3, 4, 5

INDEX